Living the Lord's Prayer Day By Day

Living the Lord's Prayer Day By Day

✦

A Pilgrimage of Faith and Action

Wilson Wayne Grant, MD

iUniverse, Inc.

New York   Bloomington

Living the Lord's Prayer Day By Day

A Pilgrimage of Faith and Action

Copyright © 2008 by Wilson Wayne Grant, MD

All rights reserved. No part of this book may be used or reproduced by any means, graphic, electronic, or mechanical, including photocopying, recording, taping or by any information storage retrieval system without the written permission of the publisher except in the case of brief quotations embodied in critical articles and reviews.

All scripture quoted in this book is from the New International Version of the scriptures (Copyright, International Bible Society, © 1973, 1978, 1984) unless otherwise noted. Used by permission of Zondervan. All rights reserved.

iUniverse books may be ordered through booksellers or by contacting:

iUniverse
1663 Liberty Drive
Bloomington, IN 47403
www.iuniverse.com
1-800-Authors (1-800-288-4677)

Because of the dynamic nature of the Internet, any Web addresses or links contained in this book may have changed since publication and may no longer be valid. The views expressed in this work are solely those of the author and do not necessarily reflect the views of the publisher, and the publisher hereby disclaims any responsibility for them.

ISBN: 978-0-595-50994-2 (pbk)
ISBN: 978-0-595-50178-6 (cloth)
ISBN: 978-0-595-61725-8 (ebk)

Printed in the United States of America

Dedication

To the staff of Laity Lodge
for providing a time and place
to meet God in a fresh and deeper way

The Lord's Prayer

or, as it is sometimes called,

The Disciples' Prayer

Our Father which art in heaven, hallowed be thy name.
Thy kingdom come. Thy will be done on earth, as it is in heaven.
Give us this day our daily bread
And forgive us our debts as we forgive our debtors.
And lead us not into temptation but deliver us from evil.
For thine is the kingdom and the power and the glory forever.
Amen.

(Matthew 6:9–13 (KJV))

Contents

Preface

It was late. The lights in most of the dorm windows had flickered out, and Howard Payne Hall was quiet—a situation that seemed to occur only after midnight. But the eight of us gathered in Jimmy's room were wide awake. We sipped soft drinks and continued a conversation that had begun in our biology class the day before.

"All this about man being just a naked ape ..." Mike yawned. "... I guess it could be true—but I really don't want to believe it. I always felt I was a little more significant than that."

"Well, when I was a freshman, I thought I understood everything," Sam added. "But now, I'm not sure."

"Who am I? What's life all about anyway?" I thought out loud. I was thrusting this question at myself as much as at anyone else. Like Sam, I used to have at least some of the answers about myself and my world. But now that I was about to graduate, myriads of new ideas were being flung at me. Some were hard to digest. Some seemed to contradict the world I knew as I was growing up.

"Maybe that's not the question at all," Arnold replied. "Isn't the proper question, 'What am I?'" He paused thoughtfully. "It seems that we moderns are finding that man is not a *who* but a *what.*"

I was sitting on the windowsill and staring out at the stars that flickered all across the November sky. The mystery and vastness of the heavens stirred my own longing to know who I was and whether I really counted for anything in this vast universe.

Who am I?

What am I?

What's life all about?

As I have viewed the paradox of my own existence, I have recognized a crying need to know who I am, where I came from, and where I am going. During that late-night rap session in Jimmy's room, I realized that I was not the only one searching for answers to such questions. Now that I am much further along the trail of life, I realize that these fundamental questions of human existence may be asked in many ways. It seems that each generation—certainly each individual—must ask these questions anew. Near the dawn of recorded history, Job asked, "What is man that you should make so much of him?" (Job 7:17). Later, David wondered, "What is man that you are mindful of him?" (Psalm 8:4). We today are asking these same questions with even more urgency as we sense the failure of culture to give meaning and substance to our daily lives. However we phrase the questions, they must be asked by each person at some stage of his or her life.

These questions have driven me to explore the roots of my Christian faith. It is through the window of prayer that I have been able to see the meaning of this faith more clearly. In that exploration, nothing has been as enlightening as meditating on the Lord's Prayer.

Through the centuries, men and women have found peace, reassurance, hope, and challenge in the Lord's Prayer. These words, few in number yet so powerful in spirit, are among the most quoted in the history of man. Recognized around the world, the Lord's Prayer is lovely in its cadence, profound in its simplicity, and moving in its power. It has, over the years, challenged serfs and humbled kings.

Growing up in the center of the Christian tradition, I easily succumbed to the temptation to take for granted the familiar words of the Lord's Prayer. Too often, in both private and public worship, I would mumble the words but hardly notice their impact. There came a time in the middle of my life, however, when the prayer's simplicity and depth captured me. I began to read it, think it, pray it, letting the words soak into my soul. I sought to pray the words in my heart, earnestly seeking to let their meaning speak for me. Along the way, I noted my thoughts and reflections in a journal. This book of meditations grew out of those reflections recorded over several years. I do not share these reflections because I have arrived at the ultimate destination of prayer; I write as a testimony to the longing I share with so many others to know the ultimate meaning of life and to find answers to the questions we chewed on in that dorm room so long ago.

My hope is that those who read these reflections will be stimulated and encouraged to meditate further on the Lord's Prayer and explore its meaning for their own spiritual journey. Certainly, one can have no better companion on the earthly journey than the Lord's Prayer, or the Prayer, as we often refer to it in these meditations.

This book may be read in any number of ways. Some will find it most meaningful when read as a part of their regular devotions. Others might want to read through the sections at one or two sittings. Others may read and reread portions of the book in order to be reminded again of the power of the Lord's Prayer to impact their lives. However the reader uses it, I pray this book of meditations will crack the door open a little, permitting fresh rays of God's light to illuminate the reader's spiritual path.

Chapter One
I Need Help

Spiritual Anemia

Then Jesus declared, "I am the bread of life. He who comes to me will never go hungry, and he who believes in me will never be thirsty." (John 6:35)

"John is just not himself," his mom informed me as soon as I sat down beside her in the examining room. "He's listless and irritable. And he doesn't eat too well either. I'm just worried about him."

I studied the two-year-old toddler cowering fearfully in his mother's lap. He did not have as much energy as the typical toddler, I thought. Gingerly examining him, I found few outward signs of illness. However, he did look a little pale, I observed.

"So John doesn't eat very well?" I asked.

"I have been worried about that," his mother replied. "He doesn't like solid foods. He just wants his bottle."

"How much milk does he drink in one day?" I continued to follow a faint diagnostic lead.

"He really likes his milk—he drinks a lot," she figured.

"We need to get some tests," I said as I called for the technician.

The diagnosis of iron-deficiency anemia was confirmed after a short wait. John's hemoglobin count was nine grams, well below the eleven or twelve which is normal for a child his age. A look at the red blood cells on a glass slide nailed the diagnosis of iron deficiency. A quick analysis of his diet showed that his intake of iron-rich foods was definitely inadequate. Once the diagnosis of nutritional iron-deficiency anemia was certain, John's treatment was obvious. I prescribed a daily dose of iron and discussed with his mother how to improve the quality and balance of his diet. When I saw John a few weeks later, his hemoglobin was a healthy twelve grams. He was a thrashing ball of energy, and his mom reported he was happier and more attentive in his play.

As I sat in the hospital cafeteria fingering a lukewarm cup of coffee after my encounter with John and his family, I reflected on what had been generally a hectic, pressure-filled day. I recalled John's anemia. Like a jolt of lightning bolting from behind a cloud on a stormy day, a new thought pierced several layers of my professional self-assurance. John's anemia was a parable of my own life. My spiritual blood had become thin and pale. No doubt, I was suffering from spiritual anemia. The symptoms were subtle: mental lethargy, impatience, intolerance, lack of emotional stamina to deal with the usual daily crises, and a general sense of uneasiness.

John's anemia was a parable through which God was speaking to me. John became anemic due to a lack of regular intake of the right foods. My spiritual malaise was due to a lack of regular intake of the right amount and quality of spiritual food. I discussed my distress with a good friend who, as a minister to students, had an office near the hospital.

Bill Hailey was a model to me of spiritual energy and sensitivity. I had witnessed his care and concern for students and patients in our medical community. I had observed with inspiration as he and his wife suffered through a family tragedy but were nurtured in their faith rather than embittered by the experience. Bill shared with me that his own spiritual energy came through daily prayer and meditation. He then did a simple but life-changing action: He gave me a copy of Oswald Chambers' book, *My Utmost for His Highest*.

Bill's witness helped me realize that the spiritual nutrients most lacking in my life were personal devotion and contact with God which came through prayer, Bible study, and meditation. Oswald Chambers spoke directly to my need for daily spiritual stimulation and nurture. He jolted me when he said, "Prayer does not fit us for the greater works; prayer is the greater work."

As I delved into Bible study, I was intrigued by the life of Jesus. I was struck by how important prayer and meditation were to him. Over and over, I read of him pulling away from very busy responsibilities for prayer and thoughts of God. Mark gives a typical report: "Very early in the morning, while it was still dark, Jesus got up, left the house, and went off to a solitary place, where he prayed" (Mark 1:35). As I took a hard, honest look into the depths of my soul, I thought, If Jesus with his unique relationship to God found prayer important, then I need it even more. And if Jesus with all the responsibilities and demands made on him could regularly find time for prayer, then certainly I can also.

My experience with John happened years ago when I was a young resident doctor. The lesson I learned from the parable of his life has been ever with me as I have grown into, and past, middle age. The mentoring of Bill Hailey and others pushed me to look beyond myself. The time spent sitting quietly in my study, reading from the Bible, asking for forgiveness, praying for guidance, planning my schedule, and praying for friends, coworkers, and patients has become the most meaningful part of my day. When this commitment has been an integral part of my life, I have been a better husband, father, physician, and friend.

Growing and implementing a prayer and devotional life that works for me has been a journey which is still in progress. I have tried a variety of techniques, times, places, and sequences. I have found that some things which worked for others worked for me too. I found other techniques that did not work for me. Prayer and meditation are intimately personal, and we must each discover the style which meets our needs. To live fully, however, we must discover—and journey toward—this personal, ongoing relationship with God.

At first, I strove for the "perfect devotional life" and was frustrated when I did not immediately have it—that magic feeling, that sense of epiphany. I know from experience that I do not always feel like praying and I certainly do not always feel God's presence—nor do I always have a warm feeling deep inside. I now realize that striving for the perfect relationship was taking me away from the relationship, the simple act of pausing before God. What counted was my offering of myself to him and spending time in his presence. The joy grows out of the effort itself; the joy is in the journey, not reaching some goal of perfection. The joy has been in discovering those things that work and those that do not work for me in prayer and devotion.

At those times when I have descended into spiritual laziness, I have tried a quick fix via a spiritual transfusion such as a monumental worship experience or a quiet weekend retreat. While such resuscitation efforts have been helpful, maybe life saving at times, I found that they, by themselves, are not sufficient to deal with my spiritual anemia. As a physician, I know that the healing of iron deficiency anemia comes slowly through sustained effort. One dose of iron, regardless of size, would not keep John well. He needed regular, daily bites of the proper nutrients. So it is also true for my spiritual anemia. Daily nurture is required.

So I am led back to the truth espoused by the apostle Paul: "Pray without ceasing. In everything give thanks: for this is the will of God in Christ Jesus concerning you" (1 Thessalonians 5:17–18).

So at this point, I was drawn into the request spoken by that disciple long ago: "Lord, teach us to pray!"

Learning to Walk

Not that I have already obtained all this, or have already been made perfect, but I press on to take hold of that for which Christ Jesus took hold of me. (Philippians 3:12)

Not long ago, I watched with pleasure as my young granddaughter toddled to her feet in her irrepressible attempts at learning to walk. It was a fascinating, hilarious, and instructive process. It was obvious that learning to walk is not an instantaneous happening; it is a process with stops, starts, tumbles, and bruises.

The process began as her parents held her up, letting her little feet bounce against the tabletop. Soon, she was pulling up haltingly to a chair, the wall, or her father's leg. Later, her father stood her on his shoes and by taking little steps illustrated what walking was all about—getting from here to there. She gingerly, tentatively took a step and sat down. Within a short time, with her mother holding her hand, she took a couple of wobbly steps on her own. She laughed and clapped with delight. Sometimes she would stumble and fall. She would cry a little, but usually when she looked up to see her mom's confident smile, she would rise to her feet to try again.

Soon, she wanted to follow her mom or dad wherever they went. Her little steps could not keep up with theirs, but they would walk slowly so that she could stay in step. Her dad could have picked her up and strode swiftly to his destination. But to do so would defeat a key purpose of her life—which is to walk on her own.

Reflecting on this process, I realize it tells me a great deal about God and how he works with us. God wants grown, mature men and women in his kingdom who can walk. For this reason, he does not carry us where we need to go. Instead, he stimulates us to walk, giving us time and opportunity to learn on our own. He wants us to grow and develop spiritually just as the child must grow and develop physically. We may wobble and fall, but he smiles and helps us get back on our feet.

God could pick us up and put us down at our destination—eternal rest, perfection, total fulfillment, heaven—but that is not what he wants for us. We are not created as robots; we are created as children with the drive and opportunity to grow, to become, to be more than we are. Each day I live, I am more aware that the real excitement of life is the journey itself—the act of becoming. The process of learning and growing is what prepares us for God's kingdom. Changing, becoming, and growing are what life is about. The scriptures assure us that this journey, this struggle to be what God created us to be, will go on until we are in heaven. Thus we have this continuing need for the spiritual nurture that we find in prayer.

For me, this journey toward self-awareness and fulfillment has not been one uninterrupted straight line. Just as learning to walk is not a simple, one-time experience for the toddler, my spiritual journey has consisted of many stops, starts, and detours, as well as occasional backtracking. When I have wandered away from God's purpose, he has put me back on the trail of life, but he seems to put me back at the point where I got off.

Some toddlers seem to master walking quickly with minimal effort; for others, it is a long, tentative process. So it is with one's spiritual journey. Some are more capable of risking than others. There are some who seem to move only inches in the journey of self-discovery and fulfillment during their whole lifetime. Then there are others who gallop forward, becoming beacons for the rest of us.

I find that I am often so hung up on seeing the imperfections in others that I do not see my own incompleteness. What did Jesus say? "Why do you look at the speck of sawdust in your brother's eye, with never the thought of that great plank in your own?" (Matthew 7:3 (*New English Version*)). As we grow to be more like Christ, as we mature in our experience and understanding of grace, we grow also in tolerance, in understanding, and acceptance of others' imperfections. At the same time, we are less tolerant of our own incompleteness.

Fortunately, God does not judge us on the basis of where we started our journey. He does not even judge us on how close we are to our eventual goal. Rather, he judges us on the basis of whether we are going in the right direction. Are we further into blind alleys, or are we headed out into the open road of life? I know that in prayer, I am a toddler stumbling and falling as I seek to grow in my understanding. God is pleased with our every effort. He is delighted when we push up, stand, and take those wobbly steps. So we are at the same place as the disciple who approached Jesus with a most relevant request.

***

Lord, in my rush to be somewhere other than where I am, in my drive to be someone other than who I am, I easily lose that sense of wonder. May the awe of your Spirit envelop me. I praise you for the love that created me. I don't understand why you made me in your image. But I cannot escape your fingerprints on my soul. Help me to discover the meaning and purpose of my being.

Chapter Two
A Haunting Thirst

I'm So Glad You Asked!

One day Jesus was praying in a certain place. When he finished, one of his disciples said to him, "Lord, teach us to pray, just as John taught his disciples." (Luke 11:1)

The biblical narrative is terse, dramatic, and to the point. These few words setting the scene for the dialogue on prayer paint, in a few broad strokes, a vivid portrait of character and action. We can only imagine the details of this drama. In my imagination, I see Jesus and his most intimate friends sitting around a small fire over which they have cooked a simple meal. Their casual banter turns to deeper things, and finally, one of the disciples, acknowledging the words Jesus just prayed over the food, makes his request, "Lord, teach us to pray." In my mind, I see the disciple who speaks for the group turning toward Jesus earnestly anticipating the answer.

I picture Jesus, his eyes twinkling, gazing into the fading sunset with a smile on his face. In my vision, he speaks softly as he whispers to himself, "This is the moment I have been waiting for!"

Of course, my fantasy is pure speculation. We do not know the actual setting of this conversation or why this particular disciple made this request at this moment. Whatever the spark that triggered the request, the disciples must have been increasingly intrigued by the praying of Jesus. They had witnessed him praying often in a variety of places and circumstances. Most of all, they saw clearly that prayer came easily and naturally to him. Along with the consistent focus on prayer, the disciples witnessed the serenity and power of Jesus' life. So it was inevitable that one of them would ask, "Lord, teach us ..."

I suspect this request excited Jesus more than any other he had heard. In fact, the reason he was here on earth, sitting in this circle of friends, was so that they would long for this kind of relationship with their creator. This request shot straight to the heart of what God was seeking to do in the incarnation when he intentionally sent his son to earth. I think it warmed Jesus' heart to hear this request, for an overarching purpose of his coming was, and is, to open the door of communion between the Father and his children. To pray was, and is, to enter into a conversation with God.

Yes, my picture of this scene is just speculation. The details of the incarnation are beyond our knowing. The scriptures simply tell us that God sent his son to earth so that his children would know him and his will for them. God's desire was (and is) that men and women would know ...

that he exists ...

that he loves them ...

and that he offers them life full of purpose and destiny.

Thus, this request on the part of one of the disciples represented a giant step in man's response to God's plan to reveal himself. To pray, then, as Jesus prayed to the Father, was to catch a glimpse of this relationship God desired to have with all men and women.

So, in my fantasy, I see Jesus turning to the disciples and saying with that twinkle in his eye, "I am so glad you asked. When you pray, pray like this ..."

A Haunting Thirst

As a deer pants for streams of water, so my soul pants for you, O God.
My soul thirsts for God, for the living God.
When can I go and meet with God? (Psalm 42:1–2)

When the unnamed disciple asked Jesus to teach him and his fellow companions to pray, he was asking for himself and his friends but he was also venting a longing deep within my own heart. He was also asking for me—and maybe for you also.

Pray, I must! I don't understand why.

I am drawn to it—to this mystery. I come to a moment when I sense that I must respond to a need, a calling, deep within my being.

I am pulled toward this thing called prayer. I have that deep thirst for something more than mere physical existence. The mundane experiences of daily life fail to satisfy this longing. I have a sense that there is more out there, beyond me. I want to know this mystery. Prayer, for me, is the reach to find *That* which is there.

I know I am not alone in this yearning. Prayer is a universal groping of all peoples in all times and in all places. In one form or another, men and women everywhere pray, even when they deny the need for it. From pagan tribesmen dancing around the fire to the supplicant on his knees in a cathedral, prayer is, and always has been, ever present in the lives of men and women. When the ruins of our prehistoric ancestors are carefully excavated and studied, amulets, beads, figures, and other artifacts of worship and prayer are prominent among the findings. Even today, the up-to-date sophisticated agnostic, immersed in scientific rational thought, can hardly help himself. When confronted with a crisis, he will likely be heard to utter an unchecked, "Oh God!"

Psychologist William James, himself no religious apologist but a keen observer of human nature, said many years ago, "We hear in these days of scientific enlightenment a great deal of discussion about why we should pray, or should not. But in all this, very little is said of the reason we do pray ... The reason why we pray is simply that we cannot help praying."[1] It is universal. Men and women, of every age and every culture, grope for something truly transcendent—something above and beyond.

I have only an embryonic grasp of prayer, but I know William James voices my heartfelt longing. Pray, I must. I may ignore it for awhile. I may forget it in the press of urgent business. But the time comes when I sense the tug, I hear the call. I hunger for prayer. Without it, I feel a vague unease, a sense of incompleteness. It is as if there is a vacuum at the center of my being straining to be filled.

So when the disciple made his request, "Lord, teach us to pray," he was truly speaking for me and, I suspect, for you.

Why Must We Pray?

Then God said, "Let us make man in our image, in our likeness ..."
(Genesis 1:26)
God saw all that he had made, and it was very good. (Genesis 1:31)

Why, then, must we pray? Why the emptiness? Why the longing to be connected with something outside and beyond ourselves? Why that sense of searching that I experienced in that college dorm so many years ago?

Is our need for prayer, for answers to these deep questions of the soul, simply a defect in our neurological architecture forged by random evolutionary forces? Is it some primitive survival instinct? Or is this a need that erupts from our intentional design by a power, a spirit, a mind, which exists outside and beyond creation as we know it?

Certainly, the great minds of history have struggled with this sense that there is more to us as human beings than mere flesh and bone. Philosophers from Plato and Aristotle to the freshest contemporary thinkers have speculated about the sense of spirit that is common to humanity. Christian saints throughout history have asked probing questions and found fragments of understanding in their own spiritual journeys.

Augustine of Hippo, Saint Augustine as we know him, writing in the fourth century challenged spiritual searchers through the ages with the raw honesty of his Confessions. He summed up his spiritual yearning in this frequently quoted passage:

> To praise you is the desire of man who is but a part of your creation. You stir him to take delight in praising you. For you have made us for yourself and our heart is restless until it finds its rest in you.[2]

Saint Augustine's confession of his spiritual restlessness speaks to a common thread running through the human experience. He certainly helps me understand my own yearning. The biblical tradition tells us that we are incurably religious because we are made that way, because of our original design. Our Christian heritage teaches that this yearning, this God-shaped vacuum at the center of our souls, was breathed into us by God who is the mind and energy behind creation. The longing for fulfillment, for the vacuum to be filled, pulls us to God, the Creator—or to a substitute for him.

Some students of the human condition try to rationalize this longing for God saying that we created God in our image to support our psychological weaknesses. They would say that God is a creature of our fertile imagination constructed to massage our anxiety over questions for which we, or our ancestors, did not have answers. Assuming this premise, they would add that since we now know more about the material facts of the universe, we no longer need the crutch of spiritual belief. However, this need, this longing, is just as real and pervasive in the human experience today as it has ever been. At the deepest level of our being, we know that there is more to this yearning than wish fulfillment. At the core of our being, we know we are incomplete. Realizing this, we hope for, we seek longingly, a sense of wholeness.

The Bible speaks to this deep longing when it affirms that indeed God created man and woman in *his* image! And at the heart of that image is a

God-shaped vacuum waiting to be filled by the presence of the Creator. Built into our very heartbeat is a yearning to know, to have contact with, the one who made us.

For those of the Judeo-Christian tradition, the Bible responds to these most profound questions. It begins by describing how God created the universe of matter and energy. Out of this matter and energy, he then created life in all of its diversity. At a critical point in this creative process, a signal happening occurs:

> And the Lord God formed man of the dust of the ground [as he had other life, but then], breathed into his nostril's the breath of life [something unique], and man became a living soul [the spirit, a part of God in us]. (Genesis 2:7 (KJV))

Something unique in the cosmos—a being with a soul, with something of God (in his image!) at its core—is revealed.

This "breath of God" infused into humankind at the creation (and into each of us at our personal creation) expands to form this vacuum that only God can fill. This vacuum is revealed to each of us through the basic needs which tug at our hearts. The longing for fulfillment of these needs drives our hunger for something more than simple satisfaction of our animal instincts. We are empty, as Saint Augustine articulated, until the vacuum is filled with the presence of God himself. The pull of these needs tugs us toward our creator. We are "restless" until these needs find true fulfillment in a relationship with God. This vacuum tugs us toward God, striving as a vacuum always does to be filled.

Thus the scriptures teach that our inner drive to pray originates in our very design and creation. George McDonald sums this up well: "They (humankind) exist that they may pray. He has chosen them that they may choose him; he has called them that they may call him—that there may be such communion, such interchange as belongs to their being and the being of their father."[3] This "interchange" is the essence of prayer.

Thus, we must search. We must pray.

Hobbled by darkness, so much of it of our own making, we can only grope for the light. But I can only believe that our yearnings after the light must be a pleasure for God to watch. I can see him saying as we grope, "Come on, move toward that crack of light there. Reach for it. Put out your hand. I am waiting to pull you to me—your Creator, your God, your Father."

The Ultimate Question

Listen to me, you who pursue righteousness and who seek the Lord: Look to
the rock from which you were cut and the quarry from which you were hewn ...
(Isaiah 51:1)

So much in contemporary culture trivializes human life and destiny:
  Existence is an accident.
  Man is a machine.
  Life is only what you make of it right now.
  Eat, drink, and be merry, for tomorrow, you will die—and be no
  more.
Our senses are bombarded with such cynicism from every direction in
today's world. The voices of entertainment, politics, mass marketing, and
the arts too often appeal to our self-centeredness and in the process seek to
convince us that "this (what we see, feel, touch) is all there is."

But in our quiet moments, in those times when we get in touch with
our inner self, we sense there is more to our life, more to our destiny, than
this momentary existence. We sense that we are more than the machine in
which we live. We are more than our day-to-day experiences. Life, somehow,
is more.

But what are we? What is our destiny? What is the meaning of our
existence? That is the question I and my friends struggled with in that college
dorm room at the dawn of our adulthood.

Also struggling eons ago with these questions, David, the shepherd and
poet who was to become king of Israel, gazed upon a starry night and called
out his own questions:

When I consider the heavens,
the work of your fingers,
the moon and the stars,
which you have set in place,
what is man that you are mindful of him,
the son of man that your care for him? (Psalm 8:34)

In these poetic musings, David does not end with his questions. He
proceeds to describe his discovery (from God's revelation) of mankind's
unique destiny—a destiny that grows out of a special relationship with God,
the Creator:

You made him (mankind) a little lower than the heavenly beings and
crowned him with glory and honor.
You made him ruler over the works of your hands;
you put everything under his feet …
O Lord, our Lord, how majestic is your name in all the earth.

(Psalm 8:5–9)

God, in his inspiration of David, affirmed that we have meaning and
purpose even as he touches us into existence. Before he created us, we were an
idea in the mind of God. He sent us into the world with purpose and intent
as Psalms reminds us in another place:

For you created my inmost being;
you knit me together in my mother's womb.
I praise you because I am fearfully and wonderfully made;
your works are wonderful, I know that full well … (Psalm 139:13–16)

Yes, as products of God's creation, we are more than the machines in
which we live. We are intentionally created to have a relationship to our
creator, and, indeed, this gives us meaning, destiny, and purpose. Life, our
life, is no random accident. Dr. Paul Tournier underscores the point: "Man
is the being to whom God speaks, with whom he thus enters into a personal
relationship. After having created the whole inorganic world, all the plants
and animals—a world blindly and impersonally subject to him—God created
man in his image; that is to say, a personal being, a partner in dialogue, a
being to whom he might speak and who could answer … whose replies he
also awaits."[4]

God made us for himself. He loves us, and he seeks to show his love in
wonderful, diverse ways. We are born into time and space as immature beings
so that we may grow in our relationship to our creator. Prayer is that open
window through which we feel the breeze of God's presence. And through
prayer, we explore the destiny God has planned for us.

***

*Father, I cannot understand creation. Nor can I fathom the depth of
meaning that explodes through the incarnation. But the wonder of your work of
love overwhelms me. It is too wonderful for me to grasp. I can only bow before
you, praising you, honoring you, and thanking you for the gift of yourself through
your Son.*

I have felt what Saint Augustine felt. I have felt the tugging of the vacuum. I have tasted the meaninglessness of trying to live my life on my own. This vacuum has tugged me into your presence. I reach out my hand, and I feel your touch. In this touch, I find my peace. In this touch, I find my destiny.

Chapter Three
What Is Prayer?

Personal Perceptions of Prayer

I will pray with my spirit but I will pray with my mind also.
(1 Corinthians 14:15)

The pull to pray is rooted deeply in our nature. But each man and woman comes to the act of prayer with varied personal perceptions and expectations. You say "let us pray" in a crowd, and most of those present will respond intuitively with bowed heads. But if those present are asked to define what they mean by prayer, most everyone would stutter with uncertainty.

When men and women of any culture explore their own personal concepts of prayer, different nuances of meaning are discernable but certain common themes predominate:

Prayer as magic. In magical prayer, the believer seeks to prod—through the right combination of acts, words, and moods—his "god" into action. The believer hopes to manipulate the god to deliver his deep-felt needs and wants: send rain, produce a good crop, heal (himself or his), or make sick (his enemy). In this scenario, the petitioner is simply asking the magician to perform a miracle. Once the wish is granted, the petitioner will be satisfied for the magician to slip back into oblivion.

Prayer as meditation. To many others, prayer is simply a means to get in touch with the cosmic power, eternal Being, Great Spirit, or Life Force. The petitioner seeks the "one" beyond himself, hoping that he will be more fully integrated as a person; he or she seeks in the "oneness" a sense of wholeness and meaning. Prayer, in this view, is a reaching out to the mystical "other" that is outside, and above, oneself.

Prayer as a psychological process. In contemporary society, prayer is often used as a form of catharsis. In this sense, prayer is a means of coming to grips with conflicting psychological forces within the person. It is, more or less, talking to oneself. Prayer becomes a way of releasing emotions and freeing oneself from the stresses of the day. One talks through, within a cloud of anonymity, his or her feelings and problems to the ultimate listening ear. After conversing with the eternal psychotherapist, one "feels" better. Because one feels better, he or she hopes life will be better.

Prayer as request. To a host of others, prayer is essentially a process of making explicit requests. More than magical chanting, this view of prayer is like a child asking a grandparent for whatever he desires. Prayer, in this view, is seeking to tap into the all-present, all-powerful force in the universe. For some petitioners, this giving force may have a concrete definition and specific name; for others, the god to whom requests are addressed is an ethereal, nebulous fate which somehow pulls the strings of the willing universe.

As these examples show, different people from different backgrounds, cultures, and needs come to prayer with diverse expectations. Whether or not these expectations are aligned with the true meaning of prayer, they point toward the universal hunger of each human being to reach beyond himself or herself to get in touch with the Presence which our deep intuition tells us exists. This hunger, itself, is a kind of prayer. But this hunger for connectedness can be easily distorted into these tangent channels which flow away from the purpose, and rewards, of real prayer.

So, what is *real prayer?*

Biblical Prayer

The Lord is righteous in all his ways and loving toward all he has made. The Lord is near to all who call on him, to all who call on him in truth.
(Psalm 145:17–19)

Prayer has always had an element of mystery about it. All efforts at prayer, even the distorted ones, hide a grain of truth. They persist in the human experience, for they represent our search for something beyond ourselves. However, all of these man-made efforts, individually and collectively, fall short of satisfying our ultimate need—the need to fill that emptiness deep within. The Bible, as a record of God's dealings with mankind, has much to say about prayer. Throughout the Old Testament—Cain's and Abel's feeble attempts to communicate with God, Moses' awe at the burning bush, David's prayer of repentance, the prophets' heartrending cries, the thanksgiving Psalms—we see mankind and God approaching each other.

In the life of Jesus, however, we see a panorama of prayer that exceeds all previous experience. Prayer was an intimate part of his daily life. He prayed with confidence as if he was speaking to someone he knew. The disciples appeared to be haunted and enticed by the spirit and power of his praying. Inevitably, one of them had to ask. So he spoke for the whole group asking, "Lord, teach us to pray."

In light of Jesus' purpose to bring God and men and women together, it is possible to imagine that Jesus did say under his breath, "I'm so glad you asked." Of course, we do not know the details of that conversation. We do know, however, that Jesus responded to this simple request with the affirmation, "When you pray, pray like this ..."

The few simple words which followed had an immediate impact on the disciples and has had a powerful impact wherever the Christian message has penetrated. As beautiful as they are in their rhythm, these few simple words illuminate the essence of prayer which is revealed throughout the scriptures: *Prayer is communication.* Prayer is personal contact with Our Creator ... Our Father ... the God! As Evelyn Underhill states, "Prayer means turning to Reality, taking our part, however humble, tentative and half-understood, in the continual conversation, the communion, of our spirits with the Eternal Spirit ..."[5]

Prayer as seen in the life of Jesus is based on an intimate, familial relationship. The purpose of prayer is a closer relationship with God so that God's will might be done in the life of the petitioner. By giving the instruction, "When you pray say ..." could Jesus be implying that he wanted the disciples to have the same relationship with God that he enjoyed? I think so.

The order of the petitions in the Lord's Prayer illustrates the priorities of Jesus' life and teaching—and certainly of his praying. The first three petitions focus on God and our relationship to him. Only then do the following three petitions deal with the needs and necessities of the one praying. God is first acknowledged and given his supreme place. Only then does the petitioner turn to himself and his needs.

True prayer, as modeled by Jesus, is never an attempt to bend the will of God to our will. Prayer is the process of submitting our will to that of God. In doing so, we acknowledge our finite nature and God's infinite being. True prayer is an interface between our earthbound minds, bodies, and souls and the eternal God. At its center, this true, honest prayer is a seeking of, and yielding to, God.

Brother Lawrence, that quiet, meditative medieval monk, who left us his personal reflections on spiritual growth in *The Practice of the Presence of God*, calls us to the very root of prayer: "I still believe that all spiritual life consists of practicing God's presence, and that anyone who practices it correctly will soon attain spiritual fulfillment."[6]

C. S. Lewis adds this injunction: "Prayer is either a sheer illusion or a personal contact between embryonic, incomplete persons and the utterly concrete Person."[7]

There is no greater joy on earth or in heaven than communion with God. Prayer, when fully realized, ushers us into the presence of that joy.

We Do Have Questions!

"My God, my God, why have you forsaken me?" (Mark 15:34)

There may have been times when we experienced prayer as personal and real. At such times, we felt God right by our sides. But each of us, at some point, will feel like the Grand Canyon separates us from God. We wonder if God is real. We have questions and no answers.

Several of us attending a couples Bible study group confronted this sense of separation as the leader asked a pointed question: "If today you met God and could ask him any question, what would you ask?" The leader started the session with this stimulating question.

Immediately, a buzz of voices filled the room. One then another of the group threw out a question. It was as if each person had been thinking about this for a long time.

As the responses were recorded on the board, the similarity was striking. Almost all the questions focused on why.

Why leukemia?

Why do bad things happen to innocent people?

Why hurricanes and tornados?

Why pain?

Why does life seem so unfair?

Why do so often the innocent suffer and the guilty go free?

Then there were a sprinkling of questions wondering how.

How did God create?

How does the atom work?

How does the brain function?

Life is full of mystery, contradictions, and surprises. If one thinks at all, one wonders. It is so very human to want to know why and how.

The questions raised by this group reflect key themes:

The existence of good and evil.

Why life seems often to be unfair.

How does it all work? What is the nature of things?

This Bible study group was studying the little book of Habakkuk. Habakkuk, we learned, was a prophet—a spokesman. As a prophet, he not only spoke for God to the people; he spoke for the people to God.

Habakkuk shouted out a list of questions:

How long, O Lord, must I call for help, but you do not listen?

Or cry out to you, "Violence!" but you do not save?

Why do you make me look at injustice?

Why do you tolerate wrong?

Destruction and violence are before me; there is strife, and conflict abounds.

Therefore the law is paralyzed, and

justice never prevails.

The wicked hem in the righteous, so

that justice is perverted. (Habakkuk 1:2–4)

Although Habakkuk lived a long time ago, his questions are strangely contemporary. They are very much like the ones our Bible study group asked. But, then, these questions have been asked myriads of times in all ages and places.

God did respond to Habakkuk's questions. But God's response was not what Habakkuk had expected or hoped for. God said:

Look at the nations and watch …

and be utterly amazed.

For I am going to do something in

your days that you would not

believe, even if you were told. (Habakkuk 1:5)

Then God added,

Write down the revelations and make it plain on tablets so that a herald may run with it.

For the revelation awaits an appointed time;

it speaks of the end

and will not prove false.

Though it linger, wait for it; it will

certainly come and will not delay. (Habakkuk 2:2–3)

God in essence said, "I am working in history; I have a panoramic perspective of things. And I am in charge." After reassuring Habakkuk that things were not as they seemed from his limited view, God added, "... the righteous will live by his faith" (Habakkuk 2:4).

We have a bare glimpse into Habakkuk's world. We have only a dim snapshot of his time and place. But his dialogue with God weaves an influential strand into our Christian heritage.

Habakkuk 2:4 was picked up by Paul and used as the text for his most definitive writings on the Christian faith, the book of Romans. In Romans 1:17, he says, "For in the gospel a righteousness from God is revealed, a righteousness that is by faith from first to last, just as it is written: 'The righteous will live by faith.'" Paul went on to explain in detail the ramifications of this faith.

Later in Romans, Paul was likely referring back to the questions voiced by Habakkuk: "And we know that in all things God works for the good of those who love him, who have been called according to his purpose" (Romans 8:28). Paul then adds with excitement, "If God is for us, who can be against us?" (Romans 8:31).

Habakkuk himself seemed to have caught a glimpse of this reassurance. Through all his questions, he maintained his faith. In the end, he says,

> Though the fig tree does not bud and
> there are no grapes on the vines,
> though the olive crop fails and the
> fields produce no food, though
> there are no sheep in the pen and
> no cattle in the stalls, yet I will
> rejoice in the Lord, I will be joyful
> in God my Savior. The Sovereign
> Lord is my strength; he makes my
> feet like the feet of a deer, he
> enables me to go on the heights. (Habakkuk 3:17–19)

Yes, we have questions. And our questions, maybe more than our faith, drive us to seek God in the act of prayer. As Christians, we have the assurance that God listens when we ask, even shout, our questions.

As we listen, we hear God's reply, "I am in charge. All things will work for the good ..."

***

Lord, like all your imperfect children, I do have questions. There is much I do not understand. Help me, like Habakkuk and Paul, to have faith to know that you care for me and that you are with me even in my questions.

Lord, I want to come into your presence as a child, but often I come as a slave only petitioning for my desires. I want to reach out to you as a child to his father. But I hold back: Am I worthy? Are you really there? Help me in my fear and uncertainty.

Chapter Four
Lord, Teach Us to Pray

Lord, Teach Us

Very early in the morning, while it was still dark, Jesus got up, left the house and went off to a solitary place, where he prayed. (Mark 1:35)

Jesus had a way of surprising his disciples at every turn. They were captivated, often mystified. The scriptures show that they were drawn to him but did not always understand him. Day after day, they saw one of extraordinary compassion, power, and stamina. He not only taught with fresh energy and insight into the human condition, but he also practiced the implications of his teachings. He listened to the heart of those he met. He responded uniquely and intentionally to their needs. He broke through social and religious barriers that had long separated peoples. He stood strong in the face of opposition that sought to destroy him and discredit what he was doing. Yet, he met every person in his path with attention and compassion. What these followers saw drove them to seek more—even as they failed to understand fully the implications of his teachings about God, the loving Father, and their relationship to him.

Day after day, the disciples saw in Jesus something phenomenal, something that opened their eyes to his source of strength:

He lived as if God were real,

and not only real, but personal,

and not only personal, but involved, concerned, caring.

These disciples saw Jesus praying daily, regularly, easily. Even a casual reading of the Gospels shows just how natural prayer was to Jesus:

He prayed routinely.

He prayed privately.

He prayed publicly.

He prayed with praise.

He prayed in thanks.

He prayed for strength.

He prayed for others, even his enemies.

The prayers of Jesus were vital—full of life—yet they were simple, personal, and expectant. God was not some faraway, vague, inanimate object. He was not an idol to be manipulated. He was real and available. He was, well, like a loving father concerned for his children.

The disciples saw in Jesus' prayers a calm, confident dialogue with this Father in heaven. It was as if Jesus was speaking to someone whom he knew—and someone who he was certain knew him. To Jesus, prayer was more than an act, more than a doing; it was a relationship.

No wonder the disciples came to ask, "Lord, teach us to pray." In asking, I believe, they were not seeking simply another religious ritual. I think they thirsted with all their being for a relationship—the same relationship they witnessed Jesus having with his father in heaven. So it was inevitable that one of them would eventually ask, "Lord, teach us to pray ..."

The Prayer

Our Father which art in heaven, Hallowed be thy name ... (Matthew 6:9)

When Jesus said to his disciples, "This is how you should pray," he opened a window through which we see rays of God's will for us. Looking through that window, we catch a glimpse of what is important in life. Jesus is not simply teaching us a new style of petitioning the deity. He is inviting all of his disciples to a more profound walk with the one who created them.

True prayer will always contain elements of mystery, for it is part of a greater mystery: the mystery of God himself and his relationship to his children. It is a mystery that calls us upward and onward—seeking, searching, hoping. When Jesus instructed his disciples to pray the words of the Lord's Prayer (or Disciples' Prayer), he started us on the journey of exploring the mysteries of all prayer. For in the Prayer, he points us toward the relationship which gives meaning to all of life.

The simple beauty and power in the Lord's Prayer has captured the hearts of men and women through the ages. Innumerable disciples as well as seekers have found comfort, peace, and direction by repeating the Prayer in their own tongue. Such reverent repetition can, and does, bring a centering to one's spiritual life which results in serenity and peace. Certainly, any of us can be enriched by voicing the words and letting the Prayer speak for us—and to us.

From the earliest days of the Christian movement, the Lord's Prayer has been an integral element in corporate worship. The repetitive use of the plural pronoun, "our," in the prayer forcefully reminds us that we are a part of something larger than our narrow world of personal concerns. Praying the Lord's Prayer in unison, together, is a powerful reminder of the familial nature of the church. Together, the followers of Christ are the "family of God." And the prayer reminds us that the church, as a living organism, is greater than the sum of its parts.

But the Lord's Prayer is more than words to be memorized and repeated. It is a stairway that leads us to a deeper journey—a journey that explores the expanding world of faith to which our heavenly Father, our Creator, is calling us. In the Prayer, we are first called to acknowledge God as our Father. Then, we are called to seek the Father's will in our life and world. Finally, we are called to acknowledge our dependence on him in all things—from asking for our daily needs to seeking ultimate forgiveness and protection. The Prayer's power is rooted in the promise that everyone can confidently approach God, who already knows each person and cares for their needs. It is this possibility of fellowship and communion which anchors the Prayer.

The Lord's Prayer is intended to be a positive illustration of how to pray rather than a mantra to quote or script to act out. Jesus does not introduce the Prayer with, "Pray just like this." Rather, he instructs the disciples to "Pray like this." In our contemporary idiom, he is saying, "Pray in the following way," or "Pray along these lines." We may begin with the simple words of the Lord's Prayer. But the words lead us to a deeper relationship with God where we can listen to his voice and send up our voice to him.

What Is Not Prayer

What do I care about incense from Sheba or sweet calamus from a distant land? Your burnt offerings are not acceptable; your sacrifices do not please me. (Jeremiah 6:20)

As Jesus modeled true prayer for his disciples, he also pointed to distortions of prayer which, at some time, tempt us all. Matthew records his words:

> And when you pray, do not be like the hypocrites,
> for they love to pray standing in the synagogues and
> on the street corners to be seen of men. I tell you the
> truth, they have received their reward in full … And
> when you pray, do not keep on babbling like pagans,
> for they think they will be heard because of their
> many words. (Matthew 6:5–8)

Jesus is addressing the temptation for public prayer to degrade into an attempt to manipulate God. We tell God what we want and expect him to deliver. Prayer under these circumstances, too easily, becomes an opportunity to show off our individual or corporate piety and spiritual worth. We must with vigilance be on our guard against such temptations. Jesus is not attacking public prayer. He, himself, often prayed aloud in public. He is making the point that meaningful prayer is not addressed to other men and women or spoken for attention and approval. Real prayer is addressed to God alone. In the end, only his approval matters. When prayer becomes simply a religious activity, when it is just a religious duty, we lose out on the real meaning and power of prayer. If we pray to impress others, we profane the purpose of prayer and we surely will not impress God.

Jesus also states that prayer is not just "many words." Prayer as modeled in the Bible is not magic incantations or hypnotic mantras used to manipulate mysterious forces of the universe. Such "vain repetitions" have no place in Christian prayer. Biblical prayer is not a ritual to be used in an attempt to control God or manipulate him into granting the wants of the one who is praying. Prayer is not a tool for getting what we want; prayer is, we remember, a personal, albeit profound, conversation between the creature and his or her creator. No magic. No manipulation.

We all, even those of us with enough experience to know better, can fall into the trap of using prayer as an attempt to coerce God into blessing our plans, our wills, our purposes. We assume that if we push hard enough, long enough that God will be obligated to bless our effort. Someone out of jest has said, "If you want to make God laugh, tell him your plans." Although said facetiously, this is a sober truth. Life will teach us eventually that we are not in charge.

Jesus' words penetrate to the center of my heart. I know I have been guilty at times of using prayer as a tool for my own selfish purposes. I have used prayer as a way of showing off my "spiritual depth." At other times of deep want, I have used my own "meaningless babble" as a magic incantation to petition for my desires from God.

More often, I profane my prayer by taking it for granted, going through the motions without taking seriously my relationship with God or focusing my attention and energies on him as I pray. In the rush of day-to-day demands, I casually acknowledge my need for God but fail to take seriously the implications of my need for him or the importance of my relationship to him. But then something in my daily experience shakes me awake. I am brought back to reality. I again hunger for prayer as modeled by Jesus.

The kind of prayer Jesus taught us is a process of communication leading to a relationship. This authentic prayer is speaking directly and personally to the God—to the Creator, to the caring Father. This possibility of fellowship and communion with a loving God forms the basis of prayer as Jesus knew it. It is this kind of prayer which he now offers his followers.

To know this kind of prayer is truly good news!

***

Lord, forgive me for those times when I have tried to manipulate you through my prayers. Forgive me for letting my prayer become mindless talk without real meaning or feeling. May I see prayer for what it is, a link with, and a true submission to, you and your will.

I am guilty of using prayer for my own ends. When I do use prayer for an ulterior reason, I am left empty. I pray that I will come to a knowledge that will let me experience the full power and potential of prayer as a way of responding to you and your presence in my life.

Chapter Five
Our Father

Our Father

But now, O Lord, thou art our Father; we are the clay, and thou our potter; and we all are the work of thy hand. (Isaiah 64:8)

Men and women of every place and time are inevitably drawn to that which is outside and beyond their own existence. Even those who protest that there is no God search for some unifying idea or force to give meaning to their existence. God, in this sense, takes on a variety of forms in the vast panorama of human imagination. He may be sun, moon, mountain, desert, spirit, Great Spirit, handmade idol, cosmic force, or philosophical concept. The truth is that all of us as human beings harbor a belief or a shadow of a belief or a hope of belief (or a rebellion against a belief) in a "god" of some fashion. But for so many, their god, however they perceive it or him or her is far away, fuzzy, and thoroughly beyond knowing.

From the beginning, the Hebrew heritage as revealed in the scriptures sees God as One: a being with personality, will, and purpose. Gradually, the picture of a God of creative energy who created from nothing all that exists is also revealed as having a loving concern for, and involvement with, the created.

This picture is painted with broad brush strokes throughout the Old Testament:

> In the beginning, God created the heavens and the earth.
> (Genesis 1:1)

Then God said, "Let us make man in our image, in our likeness." (Genesis 1:26)

So God created man in his own image, in the image of God he created him;

male and female he created them. (Genesis 1:27)

I am who I am. (Exodus 3:14)

The Lord is my shepherd, I shall not want. (Psalms 23:1)

"For I know the plans I have for you," declares the Lord, "plans to prosper you and not to harm you, plans to give you hope and a future." (Jeremiah 29:11)

This outline of the personal, loving God gradually comes into focus through the progressive story of Hebrew history. Then in the New Testament, Jesus appears, bringing color and perspective to this outline. To his listeners, Jesus asserted God was his Father and that he was also their Father. Jesus referred to God as Father more than 170 times in the Gospels. With maybe one exception, every recorded prayer of Jesus addresses God as Father. It was with this certainty of personal relationship, then, that Jesus instructed the disciples to pray, "Our Father ..."

My former pastor, Buckner Fanning, has helped me appreciate the rich meaning to be found in these words of Jesus. Every Jewish child went to bed reciting Psalm 31:5 as his bedtime prayer. They would pray, "Into your hands, I commit my spirit."

On the cross, Jesus prayed this same Psalm—but with one significant modification. In this climactic moment of his life, Jesus prayed, "Father (Abba), into your hands, I commit my spirit" (Luke 23:46). Yes, at this poignant, climactic moment, he was looking to God as his "Father."

Thus, when it came time for Jesus to teach his disciples to pray, he challenged them to address the Creator as "Heavenly Father." After all, his earthly mission was to restore their lost relationship to God and reintroduce them to their Father in heaven. (This is why in my fantasy, I hear Jesus whispering, "I'm so glad you asked," in response to the disciples' request.) Jesus affirmed this truth to the end of his ministry: "Do not hold on to me, for I have not yet returned to the Father. Go instead to my brothers and tell them, I am returning to my Father and your Father, to my God and your God," he assured the disciples after the resurrection (John 20:17).

Jesus' mission was to clear the path leading humankind to their Creator. Martin Luther reminds us that, in Jesus, God "became like us so that we might become like him." Thus when we pray "Our Father," we are making a bold statement about the nature of God. We are making an even bolder statement about who and what we are as human beings in relationship to our Creator and our God.

Our Father

I no longer call you servants, because a servant does not know his master's business. Instead, I have called you friends, for everything that I learned from my Father I have made known to you. (John 15:15)

Through the eons of human history, men and women have acknowledged a vast garden of "gods." In Greek mythology, the pantheon is populated with a myriad of deities with diverse purposes and powers. These "gods" and "goddesses" were anthropomorphic parental figures who conceived and birthed the world and its peoples into existence. In this representative pagan world view, the "gods" are pictured more like action heroes who, although frequently acting capriciously, perform feats of mythological proportions.

However, when Jesus referred to God as "Father," he referred to a quality altogether different from such anthropomorphic projections. The use of the word "Father" in the Lord's Prayer reminds us of Jesus' frequent use of the Aramaic word Abba in reference to God. The word Abba, to the people of Jesus' day, spoke of the familial tenderness and love with which the young, helpless child addressed his attentive father. It is like saying in today's idiom, "Daddy" or "Mommy." The use of this phrase by Jesus in his own prayers speaks to the special relationship of love and trust between him and his "heavenly Father."

Jesus, in the Lord's Prayer, now invites his disciples to enter into this trusting relationship and to address God as intimate Father. In doing so, Jesus introduces us to the heart of the Gospel—the good news that we have a door open to the heart of the loving God who created us and cares for us.

Theologians have, throughout history, debated the infinite ramifications of the incarnation. They continue to debate today. But for me, I rejoice in the simple fact that Jesus came to show us that God is our Father …

who brought us into being,
who loves us as children,
who wants the best for us,
who shepherds us,
who disciplines us,
who always stands near us.

I am comforted to know that the same power and cosmic intelligence which created all that exists is a being who cares for me as an individual. I can call him "Father"—yes, even more, I can call him "Abba." I can call out "Daddy" and know that I will be heard.

As Paul tells us, "For you did not receive a spirit that makes you a slave again to fear, but you received the Spirit of sonship. And by him we cry, 'Abba, Father'" (Romans 8:15).

It is this One, this loving Father in heaven, that Jesus guides us to address in prayer.

Our Father

My prayer is not for them alone. I pray also for those who will believe in me through their message, that all of them may be one. Father, just as you are in me and I am in you ... may they be brought to complete unity to let the world know that you sent me. (John 17:20–21)

Martin Luther said that the strength of the Christian faith rests in its personal pronouns. Indeed, the uniqueness of Christianity is in the personal: the personal relationships to God through his son and the family relationships we have with others in God's family. Thus we do not pray to a statue, a moon, a star, or to some nebulous object "out there." We pray to "Our Father." This first person plural, our, in the Lord's Prayer mirrors the personal relationship between us and God.

But why did Jesus use the plural, our? Why not "My Father?" In fact, a quick scan of the Lord's Prayer reveals that there is no me, my, mine, or I to be found anywhere in the prayer.

This use of "our," rather than "my," forcefully reminds us of the family nature of our relationship to God and of the corporate nature of the Christian faith. Addressing God as "Our Father" is an admission to each other that we are brothers and sisters. It reminds us that although salvation is an individual experience, the Christian life is lived out in community where we share physical and emotional space with each other as we grow spiritually.

Praying "Our Father," also reminds us that no one person or group owns God. He is Father to us all. So as we pray, "Our Father," we are acknowledging our "connectedness" to our brothers and sisters of the human family as well as our connectedness to God. The closer we draw to God and his kingdom, the closer we draw to our fellow human beings who are also seeking to know God in a deeper way. This sense of family permeates the New Testament as the early disciples, energized by the Spirit, sought to live out in community the challenges thrown to them by Jesus. In the caring fellowship of the church modeled on Jesus' unconditional love, relationships with others takes on a vital quality. In the give-and-take of community, we come to comprehend more fully the value of each person as a child of God. In community, our love for each other reflects the love that God, our Father, has for all of us.

The apostle John illustrated this spirit of family at work in the early church: "We love because he first loved us. If anyone says, 'I love God,' yet hates his brother, he is a liar. For anyone who does not love his brother, whom he has seen, cannot love God, whom he has not seen. And he has given us this command: Whoever loves God must also love his brother" (1 John 4:19–21).

Paul echoes the same thought: "So it is with Christ. For we were all baptized by one Spirit into one body—whether Jews or Greeks, slave or free ..." (1 Corinthians 12:13). And Paul continues, "But God has combined the members of the body and has given greater honor to the parts that lacked it, so that there should be no division in the body, but that the parts should have equal concern for each other. If one part suffers, every part suffers with it; if one part is honored, every part rejoices with it" (1 Corinthians 12:24–26).

These two words, "Our Father," remind us again of our familial relationship to our fellow human beings. If God the Creator is Father, then we are brothers and sisters. We should treat each other as such. This spirit, when put into practice, erases those distinctions that so often separate us—race, class, health status, age, and sinner and saint. We are truly part of the family of God.

We come to God as a part of the human family. We bow before him, shoulder to shoulder with our brothers and sisters. He is our Father. He is not the private possession of any one person, one group, or one nation. We are all his children.

Who Art in Heaven

Do not let your hearts be troubled. Trust in God; trust also in me. In my Father's house are many rooms; if it were not so, I would have told you. I am going there to prepare a place for you. And if I go and prepare a place for you, I will come back and take you to be with me that you also may be where I am. (John 14:1–4)

What is heaven?
Where is heaven?
Who is in heaven?
How do you get there?

I recently attended several funerals. First, it was my father who died. It was not long afterwards that we were attending the service of my father-in-law and soon thereafter my mother-in-law. This stark brush with death dramatized for me the preoccupation we have with the end of this earthly life—and the meaning of death. We mortals wonder about what is on the other side of the grave. We ask. We yearn. We want desperately to know that "something" will be there when we reach beyond this life. For some, this hope is only a faint, fuzzy dream. For a few, the hope of heaven is only conjecture; they are skeptical about any existence beyond this life. For others, the hope and anticipation of heaven is a solid, very real promise. However we visualize it, heaven remains, for most of us, largely a tantalizing mystery.

Even those who anticipate heaven with expectation feel more than they know about heaven. We sense from somewhere deep in our center that there is "heaven," even when our minds question and doubt. There is something in us yearning for immortality and life beyond the shadow of death, even when we cannot articulate rationally what our hope and yearning means.

The Bible shows us only veiled, misty glances of heaven but affirms that our existence goes on after physical death and that a place of completeness and fulfillment does exist. The Bible affirms that heaven is a place where life continues with meaning and creativity for those who have started on a journey with God. The inviting word pictures of heaven painted for us in the scriptures tantalize but they never clearly come into focus. The biblical language whets the appetite with these distant pictures of what is to come.

We are forced to admit that heaven is so much more than we can perceive or understand. But the one thing which makes the thought of heaven so magnetic in our Christian world view is that, above all other attributes, heaven is that place where God is! Heaven, in the biblical accounts, radiates with the wonderful presence of God and his creative energies.

Even as I am attracted to the thought of heaven as the place where God is, I am also frightened. The mystery of the presence of God is overpowering! Can I stand it? But then I am reassured that it is our Father who is there. It is the "Abba" father of Jesus' prayers who reaches toward us from heaven with welcoming hands.

The Lord has pulled away the curtain of heaven only a little. But he has assured us that ...

heaven is ...

and

heaven is where he is ...

and

heaven is where his children will eternally be with him!

The witness who wrote the book of Revelation declared: "Then I saw a new heaven and a new earth for the first heaven and the first earth had passed away, and there was no longer any sea. I saw the Holy City, the new Jerusalem, coming down out of heaven from God, prepared as a bride beautifully dressed for her husband. And I heard a loud voice from the throne saying, 'Now the dwelling of God is with men, and he will live with them'" (Revelation 21:1–3).

The ultimate comfort of heaven is that we will bathe in the presence of God, the Father, to whom we pray.

Indeed, could it be that it is God's presence, itself, which makes heaven, heaven?

Hallowed Be …

You are worthy, our Lord and God, to receive glory and honor and power, for you created all things, and by your will they were created and have their being (Revelation 4:11)

Hallowed!

Hallowed is not an everyday word in our contemporary vernacular. It is a foreign-sounding word from ages past which we moderns utter only in the Lord's Prayer. The very sound of it calls us to pause and reflect. We feel its imperative tone even when we do not fully understand it.

If we look back to discover what our forefathers were expressing in the verb to hallow, we see that it conveys such thoughts as:

to revere

to sanctify

to venerate

to honor

to make holy.

All of these verbs point to a sense of distinction, uniqueness, and reverence.

The Christian faith is rampant with paradoxes. But the greatest paradox of all is the revelation that God, the mind and energy of creation, is also our Father who cares for each of his creatures in a personal way. "Hallowed be thy name …" is our acknowledgment of this greatest of all paradoxes: God who made all that is also is the one who knows us by name.

He knows you and me even before we are born:

"For you created my inmost being; you knit me together in my mother's womb ..." (Psalm 139:13)

And he continues to care for us even now:

Are not two sparrows sold for a penny? Yet not one of them will fall to the ground apart from the will of your Father. And even the very hairs of your head are all numbered. So don't be afraid; you are worth more than many sparrows. (Matt 10:29–30)

The reality of this personal relationship is at the heart of the Christian Gospel. Yet this Father is God—the Alpha and Omega, the beginning and the end, the mind and power flinging the billions of galaxies into endless space.

The wonder of God became very real to me as I stood on a mountain in West Texas. My wife and I were in a group observing the night sky in the cool, crisp air of the Davis Mountains. It seemed as if we could reach out and touch the uncountable stars punctuating the night sky above us. Shivering in the cold, we were nevertheless fascinated as the astronomer from the McDonald Observatory discussed what we were seeing. Looking across the massive dome of sky above us, I was numbed by the sheer numbers of individual stars and their constellations.

"It is so massive, so dominating," someone said from the middle of our group.

"Most people don't realize," the astronomer responded, "that everything visible to our eyes tonight, except for one star (Andromeda) is in the Milky Way, the galaxy in which we live." Pausing for a moment, he added, "And there are as many galaxies, actually even more, beyond the Milky Way as there are stars visible to our naked eye right now. Each of these other galaxies contains as many, or more, stars as our Milky Way."

As his words bored into my mind, I felt a deep urge to kneel and pray. The God who flung these galaxies into distant space and who is even now sustaining this terribly complex cosmos is our Father. Yes, indeed! How awesome! How profound! How infinite! God created it all and holds it all together by his power and grace. A God who does all that and still loves intimately is surely good news! This awareness gives so much more meaning to Jesus' words, "Our Father who art in heaven, hallowed be thy name ..."

So, how do we "hallow" the name of God? Is this something we do by mouthing holy words in public worship and private prayer? As I think about this and read what the saints of the past have said, I realize that verbal worship and acknowledgment is important, but to hallow God's name implies much more. Most of all, we hallow his name when we live in such a way that the totality of our lives brings honor to God and leads others to him. When our thoughts, motivations, and actions magnify God's love, his name is honored. Yes it is, "hallowed …"

In this day of materialism with its emphasis on the visible and the practical, we easily lose sight of the holy. Few things awe us today. We desperately need to stand at Moses' side and hear: "Take off your shoes for this is hallowed ground." This challenges us to say with our hands as well as our mouths, "Yes, hallowed be his name."

And, thus, we can all pray:

My God, my Creator, my Redeemer, my Father, I hallow your name:

I revere,

I sanctify,

I venerate,

I honor,

I make holy in my life … your name.

… *Thy Name*

"Do not come any closer. Take off your sandals, for the place where you are standing is holy ground." (Exodus 3:5)

God is "Our Father in heaven!" Yet, he is more.

He is the same being who created by simply speaking. He flung the cosmos with the billions of galaxies into existence with a word: "In the beginning God created the heavens and the earth …" (Genesis 1:1).

The God of the Lord's Prayer is the spark of the big bang. He is the force accelerating, yet holding together, the expanding universe. He is the energy of light, time, and space. He is the gravity of solar systems, galaxies, and quasars. He is also the quantum force of subatomic particles binding all matter together. He is the artist of the blazing sunset; he is the composer of the baby's laugh.

And yet, at the strangest moment in time, he stepped beyond the role of creation to come (in the form of his son) to us:

In the beginning was the Word, and the Word was with God, and the Word was God. He was with God in the beginning. (John 1:1)

The Word became flesh and made his dwelling among us. We have seen his glory, the glory of the One and Only who came from the Father full of grace and truth. (John 1:14)

Yes, the great paradox of the Christian faith is the incarnation: the God, the force, the power who created all with a word bends down to eye level with the created and says, "I am your father. I love you. I love you so much that I will give myself for you."

Indeed, few things awe us, we the sophisticated moderns. But in spite of our self-sufficiency, we are suddenly stopped by an amber leaf floating on the ripples of a forest stream. We are enraptured by the sight of a sunset in summer or the sweet perfume of a rose in autumn. We are captivated by a new baby making eye contact for the first time. We are touched as a friend listens with intent to us. At such moments, we do feel a twinge of awe; we sense something "other," something greater, something beyond. We sense something of the sacred which points us to God and calls us again to "hallow" the name of the Creator. Deep in our soul, we are struck by the reality of that Someone greater than we.

We use many names to delineate the person of creation. For us as Christians, he is a person, not just some nebulous force. We may say,

Creator,

God,

Lord,

Master,

Eloheim ….

But none of our words circumscribe the person of God. We use many words, for he is above and beyond all our words, all our understanding. We cannot put the God of creation, the God of redemption, in a box. He is greater than our power to define him. Thus we hallow, hold holy, bow down to God—whatever name we employ to point to him.

To hallow his name, then, means that we recognize God for all that he is and that we make our hearts his temple, his dwelling place. "Hallowed be thy name" is the petition which saves the concept of God as Father from careless, sentimental emotion. Focusing and meditating deeply on the power and the grace of God, our Father, our Savior, our Creator, we reach for his outstretched hand. But we remember his power and majesty. We "hallow" his name.

***

Lord, before the flaming bush of rekindled spirit, I take off my shoes—for I am on holy ground. I am in your presence. May my outward walk mirror an inward reverence for you. Let thy name be hallowed in me so that others may see you and be drawn to you.

O Lord, in a world so full of hell made of man's harm and hurt, of man's failure and frustration, I want to know that heaven exists and that goodness does reign there. Deep within me is a longing to know that behind the uncertainty of life, there is purpose, hope, and destiny.

Chapter Six
Thy Kingdom Come ...

Thy Kingdom

"The kingdom of heaven is like a treasure hidden in a field. When a man found it, he hid it again, and then in his joy went and sold all he had and bought that field ... Again, the kingdom of heaven is like a merchant looking for fine pearls. When he found one of great value, he went away and sold everything he had and bought it." (Matthew 13:44–47)

Anyone who has attended church with any frequency knows that the word gospel is derived from a Greek word meaning "good news."

We first hear it at the birth of Jesus as the angel shouts, "I bring you good news of great joy ..." But then the word gospel appears over one hundred times throughout the New Testament. When Matthew, Mark, Luke, and John penned their records of Jesus' life, these writings were quickly called "the Gospels" by the early Christians.

So, what makes this gospel good? What makes it good news?

What made it good news to those shepherds that night at the birth of this inconspicuous baby?

Why was it good news to the throngs who listened to Jesus on the hillsides of Galilee?

Why was it good news to the early disciples who often suffered great hardships because of their adherence to this "gospel"?

Certainly, the people who first heard of this "good news" and were captivated by it came from all walks of life but most were not privileged. Most were poor farmers, merchants, and fishermen eking out a bare subsistence from stony fields and stormy lakes. Many were outcasts of one kind or another. A few, like Zaccheus, while more affluent, were mentally and spiritually restless. For most, life was not easy. There was plenty to worry about. Burdensome taxes, the iron-handed rule of the Roman military government, and hard work were regular parts of their lives. But Jesus also said that he brought good news to the affluent—the Roman rulers and those who profited from working with them. His message and life was good news to the righteous as well as the less fortunate.

Yes, what did this man Jesus have to offer that would be good news to these diverse groups of humanity?

More important, today, what is there about this "gospel" that is good news to us who are buffeted by the many contemporary anxieties and cosmic worries? This question is more urgent as we seek to chart our way in this post-Christian era.

There was a time in my own life when I was saying, "Jesus is not all that relevant to me." I did not see anything about him that made me feel particularly good. I was searching for meaning and direction to my life, but it eluded me.

Then I met Nat Tracy.

Dr. Nat Tracy was a professor of religion and philosophy at Howard Payne University when I was a student. He was a big man with soft eyes and billowy gray hair. His voice rose with emotion and his hands waved excitedly as he talked of the subtleties of man and God. He did not teach a cookbook, rote religion. He asked questions. He made you think. For Nat Tracy, combining religion and philosophy was as natural as breathing. Religion gave meaning to philosophy. From his own deep devotion, he knew that the Christian faith answered the questions that the philosophers were asking.

The moment that changed my life occurred one spring morning at the beginning of New Testament class. Dr. Tracy strode to the front of the class and, as always, began the session with a one-sentence prayer. That day, the prayer was, "Lord, help us today to know that which makes the Gospel good."

This simple prayer shook me out of my malaise and launched me on a lifelong search to discover "that which makes the Gospel good."

It seems to me that the early church fathers got it right when they gathered together the recordings of Jesus' life and teachings, bound them together, and called them "the Gospels." The Gospel grows out of the life of Jesus—what he taught us about God and, even more important, what he showed us about God.

Confronted by this Jesus of the Gospels, I have come to see that the Gospel is good news for the following reasons:

The Gospel is good news because Jesus tells us that the God who created the universe, like a father, is interested in us as persons and has a purpose for our existence.

The Gospel is good news because Jesus tells us that the God who created us loves us enough to accept us before we are acceptable.

The Gospel is good news because Jesus tells us that God offers unconditional forgiveness and an opportunity for a new beginning through the mystery of the cross.

The Gospel is good news because Jesus tells us that once he has touched our lives, he and the Father who created us will not leave us but will walk with us through life's journey and into eternity.

One of my Sunday school class members tells of walking about her (Christian) college campus and hearing a street preacher rail at those passing by, "The end is near; escape eternal damnation."

There must be more to the Christian message, she thought.

Sometime later, she read in Matthew: "From that time on Jesus began to preach. 'Repent, for the kingdom of heaven is near.'" It came to her that the kingdom of heaven is not a threat but a gift of God to us. The kingdom of heaven is the presence of God. The ultimate message of the Gospel, that which makes it good, is that the God of all, the Creator, is near. He is with us, ready for us to reach out and feel his touch.

I have long been comforted and challenged by one of Jesus' most dramatic promises recorded in the tenth chapter of John: "I have come that they might have life, and have it to the full" (John 10:10). This is comfort; this is hope; this is challenge; this is good news! Once I have allowed Jesus to kindle the fire of new life (the new birth) in me, he persists in throwing fuel on the fire, and he provides me with his Spirit to guide and teach, support, and affirm. "And I will ask the Father, and he will give you another Counselor to be with you forever—for he lives with you and will be in you. I will not leave you as orphans; I will come to you" (John 14:16).

Jesus broke the vicious cycle of frustration, drudgery, and hopelessness that smothered my life. He tells me that I am of ultimate worth, whatever my present failings and misfortunes may be. He tells me that he will stick with me until some sense and meaning is woven into my life. That, for me, is good news.

This Gospel, the Good News of the kingdom of God, is available to every person.

... *Come*

What I mean is that God was in Christ reconciling the world to himself, no longer holding men's misdeeds against them, and that he has entrusted us with the message of reconciliation. We come therefore as Christ's ambassadors. (2 Corinthians 5:18–20)

A king is one who reigns—who has power, authority, and influence—over a place and a people. A kingdom, then, is that place where the king's wishes are honored, accepted, and obeyed. It is the place where the king's personality and will sets the tone and marks the priorities. Being a good citizen of any kingdom involves respect and obedience to the laws and commands of the king.

To pray, then, "Thy kingdom come on earth," means we earnestly seek for God's will and spirit to reign here and now, on earth, where we are. The present world with too much conflict, confusion, and darkness doesn't look anything like God's territory. Evil has gained a foothold on earth. Evil's presence is all too real. As C. S. Lewis reminds us, this world is "enemy-occupied territory."[8] But as Christians, we know that the true king has landed on earth.

Therefore, the essence of the Gospel is that God, our Creator, has reached out to the world in the coming of his son. His kingdom is coming, penetrating the strongholds of evil. Jesus spoke often of this kingdom. It is like a seed, he said, that has been planted and is now germinating, energized to grow. Our response should be to bow before God acknowledging his majesty and power in the here and now. In our submission to him, we commit to participate in this true kingdom.

Jesus makes clear that he is not speaking of nations, peoples, or territories when he speaks of "the kingdom." "The kingdom of God is within you," he points out on more than one occasion. The line separating good and evil passes not between states, classes, or political parties but right through the human heart. It is in the hearts of men and women that the great battle between God's kingdom and the kingdom of evil is fought. The kingdom of God comes on earth as men and women submit their wills to God and accept God's reign in their lives. Praying "thy kingdom come" means opening our own heart and soul to the presence and leadership of God. To speak of the kingdom is to confront our inner self with the personal challenge of accepting or rejecting the will of God.

Jesus promises that the kingdom of God will not come as an army of brute force. It will come secretly, even silently, but relentlessly. It spreads like the yeast permeating the bread dough from the inside out, forever changing its nature. "The kingdom of heaven," he said, "is like yeast that a woman took and mixed into a large amount of flour until it worked all through the dough" (Matthew 13:33).

This petition, "Thy kingdom come," is not simply a hope that something will happen to the world in which we are spectators. It is a commitment to be active participants in the coming of that will and purpose. It means that we intentionally give our heart to God's presence and rule.

As we pray the Lord's Prayer, we affirm we are ready to experience the kingdom with all its love and grace of God. That grace, when it comes, will make each of us a new creature and challenge us to live out the will of God. Thus, this is not a prayer for staying the way we are. It is a leap toward growth, toward becoming, toward the kingdom.

With this challenge to the disciples of the first century, as well as to those of all times and places, Jesus offered a destiny rich in significance and meaning. We are challenged to be God's visible presence to a lost, lonely, and confused world. God loves the world unconditionally. Those who would claim his name and seek to follow him are the instruments of that love.

As we honestly pray the Prayer, we are committing ourselves to being a part of the answer to the petition, "Thy kingdom come." We are committing ourselves to letting the kingdom come in us and then through us to the world around us.

As we are launched on the journey of becoming the real persons God created us to be, we are challenged to bring the sunlight of God's love to the world where we live. We cannot do this on our own; the task is larger than any one of us mortals. But as we commit ourselves to God and the work of his son, we are energized by the Holy Spirit to live out our faith day by day and to be ambassadors of the kingdom.

As we commit ourselves to the kingdom of God, we have destiny. We belong. We are a part of something infinitely larger than ourselves.

Thy Will ...

"For I have come down from heaven not to do my will but to do the will of him who sent me." (John 6:38)

The ultimate meaning of prayer can be nothing other than this: the submitting to God, saying, "Thy will be done." This yearning, then, is the epicenter of the Lord's Prayer. Its power is focused here and from this point ripples the energy of all prayer. The focal point of true prayer is bringing the created into symmetry with the Creator and his purposes in creation.

Many people, however, stall at this beginning point of prayer. They question, "Is there a will, a cosmic purpose, at all? Am I here for a reason, or am I here simply by chance?"

Some voices whisper, others shout, that there is no overarching will in the universe. All that exists is an accident of time and place. They insist that humankind with intelligence, feelings, and a sense of destiny is the product of a chance meeting of energy and matter. The universe, after all, is a great mechanism operating on auto pilot—on auto pilot because there is no actual pilot with a map or flight plan. Thus the cynics would say there is no will to seek.

But faced with such a cynical world view, most thoughtful men and women will at some point stop and ask, "Is that all there is?" There is a sense, maybe vague at times, that we are more than simply robots, driven by instincts, living in a universe without meaning.

Sooner or later, most of us, in wonder, seek personal answers to this cosmic question: "Is that all?" We sense intuitively that there is a will beyond us, that life does have design, purpose, and direction. We yearn for, we are even driven to, intimacy with That Which Is—even when we don't know It by name. We seek, I believe, because of the pull of that God-shaped vacuum within us.

Indeed, from the very first words, the Bible asserts that the cosmos has design, and thus, meaning, purpose, and direction. There is will, volition, and decision behind what is happening in the universe. Subsequently, nature moves forward with design and intention. The scriptures affirm the will behind all the happenings of the cosmos is a personal God. This God, creating with purpose, "... saw all that he had made and it was good" (Genesis 1:31). The creation was good because it fit God's intention. The rest of the Bible story is a history of God seeking to teach this creation his will and purpose.

The core of that purpose as revealed in the Bible is that God is love. God created a universe of laws in which he then placed creatures—children created in his image with a will of their own. His ultimate purpose is that these children will choose to love him as he loves them.

But for this to happen, he had to give them something of himself. ("In our image, let us make man," God states at the climactic point of the creation story.) A core part of this image is our ability to choose—thus have a will. God could have created us as robots. As robots, we would function precisely and mechanically as programmed. We would, as our program dictated, bow dramatically at the right moment and say, "I love you, O Lord." But such robots would be toys and not children. God created us as children for he wants us to choose to love him. His ultimate will is that all his children grow to the point where they openly turn toward him and shout, "Our Father in heaven, your will be done—not only in the universe but in my heart."

Thus, the essence of true prayer is the hunger of the created to find oneness with the Creator. Too often, religion is more an effort to court the favor of the god(s) through petition or magical rites. We pray mostly for God to alter our conditions. But real prayer, as we Christians understand it, means opening our mind to the mind of God so that his will reigns. The true meaning of prayer, then, is seeking and doing the Father's will. We pray more for God to change us rather than change our condition.

... Be Done

For we are God's workmanship, created in Christ Jesus to do good works, which God prepared in advance for us to do. (Ephesians 2:10)

What is the ultimate purpose of mankind?

If we ask a Christian of traditional bent, he may well reply, "To glorify God." If we ask a youth struggling for identity, he is likely to shout, "To do my own thing; to express myself."

While at first glance, the two answers appear to contradict each other, they may have more in common than we think. To have our God-shaped vacuum filled—to find our true self, to discover the meaning of our existence, to have our basic needs met—is to "express oneself" in the truest sense. According to the Bible, to have this kind of relationship also glorifies God. We have already discussed that our most fundamental, basic human needs were planted in us by God in the creative process. By virtue of the way God created us, these needs can only be completely filled by him. In fact, these needs were planted by God to draw us to him. The intended creator-creature relationship is one in which we open ourselves to God, seek to live in his presence, and commit to his purpose. This relationship not only glorifies God; it also liberates us to find that unique destiny for which we are designed. Only then do we experience ultimate joy and personal fulfillment.

The scriptures urge us to let Christ be our pattern for living. This call does not, however, imply that God intends for us to be warmed-over imitations or carbon copies. We are to be Christ-like in the sense that Christ was real, true to his purpose, and claimed his destiny. We are to be like Christ in the sense that he sought fully to do God's will. The affirmation of scripture is that each person is intentionally and uniquely designed by God. He then breaks the mold. The genetic code, unraveled by contemporary scientists, shows that we do have much in common with others, but it also points to the uniqueness of each person. Science shows that no two genetic patterns are the same, thus affirming the biblical view that each person is special. The Gospels challenge us to actualize this uniqueness. To assert oneself, to "do your own thing" is not un-Christian in the true sense of God's intention. It can be the most Christian thing. When we truly assert ourselves by humbly seeking God's will for our lives, we also honor God.

However, we must avoid the danger of an iconoclastic faith which is isolated and self-centered. Our gifts, calling, and destiny are discovered by interpreting the scriptures in the context of a shared community that gives us perspective of God's overall will and purpose. Isolated, independent interpretation of life and scripture makes us vulnerable to self-delusion and distorted vision.

Thus, to honestly pray, "Thy will be done," does not imply that we must give up our individuality. It does mean that we commit that individuality to God, allowing him to use all that we are to bring his will to pass in this time and place. As we find God's will for our lives and courageously act on that will, we discover we are doing our "own thing." Our "own thing," however, will be that which God created us to be from the beginning.

The call to follow God's will jolted the disciples after the crucifixion. Numbed at first by the sheer force of the crucifixion and the empty tomb, they were energized by the presence of Jesus. He, who had seemed so defeated, was again with them. He was the same—but also different. Yes, they were confused. Indeed, they were having a hard time sorting out the implications of all that had happened. Now Jesus was again walking with them—as he had so often in previous times. As they again gathered to talk together, he startled them with a new challenge: "As my Father has sent me, even so send I you" (John 20:21).

The disciples at first did not seem to understand what Jesus really meant. They likely pondered these words as well as many other things he said in those days. Then things changed dramatically. Jesus left them, saying he was returning to the Father. This drew the disciples together in a way they had never experienced before. Then came the time when God demonstrated the power and presence of his Spirit in a very different way at Pentecost. These once-confused men and women saw the world, themselves, and Jesus in a totally new light.

Only then did Jesus' words sink in. The implications were now starkly real. They realized that Jesus was, in essence, saying, "I'm no longer walking in the flesh the streets of Jerusalem, the lonely shepherd paths of Judea, or the shores of Lake Galilee. I have other tasks to complete with my Father. I will only walk the streets and the lake shores as your feet walk them. I will only touch the sick and lonely as your hands touch them. I will only feed the hungry as you care for them. I can no longer stay in this world in the flesh. I am here only as I am here in you."

How were they going to do this? They quickly realized that they could not follow in Jesus' footsteps by themselves in their own strength. They could follow him only as they called on the same resource that sustained Jesus—the relationship to God the Father through the Spirit. They came to see that they indeed represented Jesus' presence and power in their world. Acting on this assurance, they proceeded to "turn the world upside down" (Acts 17:6).

The apostle Paul would later write, "What I mean is that God was in Christ reconciling the world to himself, no longer holding men's misdeeds against them, and that he has entrusted us with the message of reconciliation. We come therefore as Christ's ambassadors" (2 Corinthians 18–20 (New English Bible)). The disciples discovered that their lives had meaning and purpose as they actively became Jesus' hands and feet. They, indeed, counted. They made a difference.

We live in a time and place that desperately needs a Gospel of Good News. But our world will be touched by the grace of God only as we are willing to be available to him. As we open ourselves to this calling, we realize our full potential. We experience life in all of its glory and meaning.

Even as we pray "thy will be done," we are challenged to bring the sunlight of God's love to the world where we live, regardless of how small that world seems to us. Our dawning personhood, which we find in the fellowship of Jesus Christ, allows us to be free to be ourselves, and to help others become free. We find God, life, and ultimate fulfillment as we burst out of our cocoon of selfishness and spread our wings of love to touch others.

An unknown author has said fittingly:

> I sought my soul,
> > But my soul I could not see.
> I sought my God,
> > But my God eluded me.
> I sought my brother,
> > And I found all three.

Dr. Frank Laubach, missionary and literacy educator, answered the question, "How do you find yourself and God?" In *Letters by a Modern Mystic*, he wrote, "So if anyone were to ask me how to find God, I should say at once, hunt out the deepest need you can find and forget all about your own comfort while you try to meet that need. Talk to God about it and He will be there."[9] How do we know we are making progress on our journey toward a full life? When we can spontaneously open up to others and genuinely love, we are getting close to God and his ultimate will. In loving and caring, we become a part of what God is doing in the universe. "We know we have passed from death unto life because we love the brethren" (1 John 3:14).

Saint Frances of Assisi, who modeled servanthood in such a profound way, challenges us in this lovely prayer remembered by so many:

O Master, let me not seek to be consoled as much as to
console,
To be understood as much as to understand,
To be loved as much as to love.
For it is in giving that we receive.
It is in forgetting ourselves that we find ourselves.
It is in forgiving that we are forgiven;
And it is in dying that we are
Raised up into eternal life.
Amen.

Exceptional in the Ordinary

"As the Father has sent me, I am sending you." (John 20:21)

We first hear of the word Gospel at Jesus' birth. The shepherds hear the angels' words, "I bring you good news of great joy that will be for all the people. Today in the town of David a Savior has been born to you; he is Christ the Lord" (Luke 2:10). This baby, and the man he became, is the physical evidence of God's involvement with us: "The Word became flesh and made his dwelling among us," the apostle John affirms (John 1:14). I am fascinated by the way Peterson translates this: "The Word became flesh and blood, and moved into the neighborhood."[10]

John goes on to remind us that God took this giant step of the incarnation because he loved us: "For God so loved the world that he gave his one and only son" (John 3:16).

As he walked the paths of Palestine, Jesus lived out this involvement. He had a way of touching, often literally, everyone he met. One of the most dramatic moments in the New Testament occurs as Jesus is confronted by a man with leprosy (Mark 1:40). By religious and civil law, this man was untouchable and prohibited from contact with anyone. Though it would have been beyond the call of duty to even speak to this man, Jesus did much more. He stopped, listened, and responded to his need. He then made a most impressive gesture—one with overwhelming significance for all who would be Christian. "Jesus reached out his hand and touched the man" (Mark 1:41). In that act of touching the leper, Jesus identified with him and his condition.

At the climax of his own intense earthly work, Jesus challenges his followers with this great undertaking, "As my father has sent me I am sending you" (John 20:21). Those early disciples and those of us who would be disciples today are called to care, to love, and to touch as Christ did. In a real sense, we are called to be partners with God in reaching out to our world as we know it in love and care. Through the ages, those committed to be followers of Christ have stepped up, seeking to follow the best they could in those big footsteps.

The early Christians went out and penetrated the world of their day with God's message of love. They were willing to reach beyond their comfort zones, ever seeking to minister to all people. They could say, "Show me your faith without your deeds, and I will show you my faith by what I do" (James 2:18). In the Middle Ages, Francis of Assisi was a stirring and reforming force, helping the church to refocus on Christianity's core values. The turning point in his life occurred when he worked up the courage to touch a leper and minister to him. At that moment, he changed from a carefree youth with all the advantages of wealth and education to one of the most unselfish persons in history. Where leprosy exists today, it is Christian missionaries who are teaching, rehabilitating, and educating. In modern times, for example, the surgical rehabilitation of lepers was pioneered at the Christian Medical Center in South India by Dr. Paul Brand and coworkers.

Not all of us are called to get involved with lepers of course. Many other conditions serve to isolate and separate members of the human family. In her book, *A Simple Path*, Mother Teresa chronicles her modern-day call to work with the poorest of the poor beginning in India and eventually all over the world. She was simply following the footsteps of many other paragons of faith: Albert Schweitzer, medical missionary to Africa; Eric Lydell, Olympic champion (of *Chariots of Fire* fame) and missionary to China; Frank Laubach, missionary to the illiterate; Amy Carmichael, missionary and rescuer of abused children in India.

All of these heeded the call of Christ to follow in his footsteps and reach and touch the world around them in his name. But they are only the visible ones. An uncountable cast of unsung heroes of the faith walk with these more visible ones.

We, the ordinary Christians, contemplate these superheroes of involvement and sigh. If only we could have such meaning in our own lives. But such extraordinary involvement, we are certain, is beyond us. We cannot go there, do that, or make that kind of difference. After some period of dreaming, we pull back into our shell of self-interest and suppress our longings under the weight of contemporary concerns. It all seems so impossible. We can't do the great things, so we just won't do much at all.

It is a shame, however, if we stop here with our dreams. We can do something. The real difference in human existence is made by the everyday man and woman doing what they can where they are. Oswald Chambers confronts us directly. "It is instilled in us that we have to do exceptional things for God; we do not. We have to be exceptional in ordinary things." Then he adds, "We are called to be unobtrusive disciples, not heroes. When we are right with God, the tiniest thing done out of love to Him is more precious to Him than ... anything else we might do."[11]

Mother Teresa challenges us to "Do ordinary things with extraordinary love."

Brother Lawrence, who lived out his life as a dishwasher in the monastery, reminds us in his little classic, *The Practice of the Presence of God*, "Never tire of doing even the smallest things for Him, because He isn't impressed so much with the dimensions of our work as with the love with which it is done."[12]

Meaningful involvement does not necessarily require a journey overseas. It means taking the love of Jesus to our world where we are now. Jesus simply said, "Love your neighbor." He may at some time call you or me to go to unusual places. Until then, we can make a difference where we are. Maybe some of us cannot change the world but we can impact our family, our block, our office, our classroom. "As my father has sent me ..." The words of Jesus ring in our ears. As we do ordinary things with extraordinary love, we are participating in God's kingdom. And in doing so, we are saying, "Thy kingdom come, thy will be done." And in doing so, we are putting feet to our prayers.

Half-Price

"If anyone would come after me, he must deny himself and take up his cross and follow me." (Luke 9:23)

The radio announcer's words shook me out of a daze. "Did he really say that?" I asked the radio in disbelief. Then the announcer repeated the advertisement for a local Christian bookstore. "Everything Christian at half the price," his voice boomed clearly.

My mind told me that these words were simply a catchy way to entice customers into this very fine store. But the words kept churning in my mind. Was this not a frank, if unintended, appraisal of our culture's attitude toward anything spiritual? While there is a verifiable awakening to religious and spiritual matters today, there is a pervasive indifference to the demands of faith.

Yes, we want our spiritual hunger satisfied—but at a discount.

We want to get closer to God—but without confronting our inner motives.

We want to help our fellow man—but we don't want to give up any of our comfort and security.

We want to be part of a church—but we don't want our church to ask much of us.

Yes, give me faith—but at half price!

We moderns want faith, but we don't want to give much for it. We want the trappings of religion, but we don't want the demands or responsibilities. This attitude is very different from the life Jesus lived and the challenge he left with his disciples. At the start of his ministry, Jesus announced his calling with clarity. Standing in the synagogue one Sabbath with some friends and family, he read from the scroll of Isaiah. "The Spirit of the Lord is upon me," he read, "because he has anointed me to preach good news to the poor. He has sent me to proclaim freedom for the prisoners and recovery of sight to the blind, to release the oppressed, to proclaim the year of the Lord's favor" (Luke 4:17). At this initiation of his work, Jesus was accepting a demanding challenge. He was not proposing a half-price approach to life.

Immediately following this declaration of his mission, he was confronted with the period of temptation in the wilderness. Central to all these temptations, so graphically described in the Gospels, is an invitation to take the shortcut to fame and fortune—to accomplish his goals the cheap way. The devil made his offer to Jesus with attractive propositions: "You have the power. Go ahead and work a miracle to satisfy your hunger and that of the people. Such a feat will really catch the attention of the crowd. You will have them eating out of your hand." Satan followed this with, "And if you really want to reach your goals quickly, do something spectacular. Just jump off the top of the temple. The people will be amazed. They will call your name in the streets." Then finally, he made his clincher offer, "If you really want to do it the easy way, just give this job to me. I will take care of your mission. Just come over into my camp."

Jesus rejected these enticements to seek the easy way. He knew, in fact, that there were no cheap shortcuts to accomplishing the purpose for which he came to earth. His purpose was not to amaze, to thrill, or to win a following at any cost. Rather his purpose was to win the hearts of men and women. To do this, he would have to love them.

Jesus saw life in terms of maximum daily opportunities, not in terms of minimum daily requirements. He went about touching lepers, healing the sick, listening to the spiritually needy, bending down to hold the little children, and standing up for the weak and oppressed. He modeled a life of commitment, involvement, and integrity.

At the end of his earthly ministry, Jesus turned to those who had been with him and said, "Therefore go and make disciples ..." (Matthew 28:19). These early disciples were numb to the meaning and challenge of these words. It took a while for the true meaning to sink in. When the disciples did realize the significance of this challenge given by their master, they went out with maximum commitment. Following in Jesus' footsteps, they did "turn the world upside down."

The bookstores are stuffed with books with titles like, *Five Easy Steps to a Successful Marriage*, *Child Rearing Made Easy*, and *Ten Simple Steps to Spiritual Maturity*. When we stop and think about it, we know such titles are sadly misleading. Anyone who has been there knows that marriage is not easy. It is hard. Child rearing is exhausting. Growing spiritually is complex, certainly not simple. (But can you imagine the sales of books with titles like, *Five Hard Steps to Marriage*, *Child Rearing Is Never Easy*, or *The One Hundred Complex Steps to Spiritual Maturity?*)

Jesus calls us to the hard (but rewarding) task of being his hands and feet and voice in the world where we live. So as we begin the Lord's Prayer with the words, "Thy kingdom come," we are committing ourselves to letting the kingdom come in us—and flow out from us to the world. The reward of taking our faith seriously, rather than seeking a half-priced bargain, is that we have destiny. We belong. We are a part of something infinitely larger than ourselves. We are a part of what God is doing in the universe.

Lost and Found

"I have come that they may have life and have it to the full." (John 10:10)

I remember a table at my grandmother's house. Sitting outside under a shed, it was beat up, cracked, and leaning to one side. Some in the family said it should be thrown away. But my grandmother said, "No, I think I can use it."

She brought it inside, cleaned it up, and had someone tighten the legs. She then oiled the wood and covered the top with a nice cloth. She found some benches, and it became the perfect table for the grandkids. Grandmother literally saved the table from the trash heap. But she also saved it to a new life and a new purpose.

When I first became a Christian, I saw my salvation as primarily an escape from something—from the "lostness" of the human trash heap called hell. My salvation was just one big sigh of relief. It was much later, after help from many fellow believers, that I came to see that in Christ we are saved to something more than saved from something. In salvation, Christ is restoring us to new life and purpose just as my grandmother restored the table to new life. We are given meaning and purpose for our life. Our true gifts are unwrapped for productive use.

As we discovered earlier, Jesus announced at the start of his ministry, "Repent, for the kingdom of God is near" (Matthew 4:17). Many a sermon has been preached from this text posing the words of Jesus as a threat. In reality, however, these words of Jesus are an invitation—an invitation to witness something life changing. It is Jesus saying, "Something wonderful is about to happen!"

Throughout the Gospels, the kingdom of God is described as a place of great value, a place to be desired, a place worthy of selling all you have to obtain it. Jesus' words are a promise that God's intention for us is more than we can imagine. Later, Jesus amplified this, saying, "I have come that they may have life, and have it to the full" (John 10:10).

Continually, through his ministry, Jesus pointed out to those who would listen what God desired for them. He challenged them with words like, "You are the light of the world" and "You are the salt of the earth."

He brought out the best of the self in those he met: Peter, the rugged, burly fisherman turned dynamic leader; Zaccheus, the rich exploiter turned reformer; Mary and Martha, ordinary folks who became true saints—all are examples of the work Christ was doing in the lives of people. Christ was in the business of unlocking the true self in those who responded to him. An honest discovery of ourselves allows us to be real persons who can make free choices. We can cut loose from the crowd and think for ourselves. We can begin to dig up and explore our original gifts and purposes.

As Craig Barnes stated,

To be found by God means more than just not being lost anymore. It means that we now have the opportunity to be restored to what God created us to be from the beginning.[13]

Paul pointed to the adventure we are on with God when he shouted, "The whole creation is on tiptoe to see the wonderful sight of the sons of God coming into their own" (Romans 8:19, Phillips).[14]

Listen to the words:

"Standing on tiptoe!"

"To see the wonderful sight!"

"Coming into their own!"

What a destiny God has for those who listen to the voice of Jesus and follow him!

Yes, to be saved is to be found. And to be found is to have the door of the kingdom of God opened to us.

***

Lord, as I pray for your kingdom to come. May I be willing to let your will penetrate my work, my play, my relationships, my dreams. It is hard for me to let go of my own selfish will. Too often, Lord, I pray to change your will, not to find it. Forgive me.

Lord, indeed, the spirit is willing but the flesh is weak. Help me to want to want to live up to the challenge of your will for my life. I am fearful that if I truly submit to your will, I will have to give up something of myself. Help me to remember today that doing your will is the most fulfilling act I can commit. Help me to seek that abundant life that you came to give. May I not settle for less.

Chapter Seven
Give Us ...

Give

And pray in the Spirit on all occasions with all kinds of prayers and requests. With this in mind, be alert and always keep on praying for all the saints. (Ephesians 6:18)

As we discussed earlier, for many people, prayer is synonymous with "praying for," or asking for, something. Asking for help is certainly a part of any parent-child relationship. Thus asking our heavenly Father for help is a natural part of the Lord's Prayer. So in the middle of the prayer, the tone shifts as Jesus instructs us to simply ask, "Give us ..."

While asking is natural, we mortals are often ambivalent about asking for anything, however. There are times when we impulsively ask God to work great magic on our behalf. We want him to massage our hurts, banish our worries, and cater to our wants.

Sometimes we treat God as a vending machine. In all colors and shapes, vending machines populate our contemporary landscape ready to attend to our need for their cornucopia of contemporary products—for a price. They cater to our modern fixation on instant gratification. We only have to put in our money, then out comes our product—instantly.

We contemporary Christians have all too easily incorporated the vending-machine mentality into our religious experience. Our expectations are great; we put our religious coinage in the proper slot, and we expect to see the desired product drop into the hopper. We put in ritual, religious talk, outward piety, and a measured monetary contribution here and there. We expect well-being, health, happiness, and success—and we expect them instantly.

Then there are times when our pride takes over and we shout, "I am the captain of my ship. Need someone? Not I!" This side of our person does not want to admit that we need anything from anyone, even God. To ask would mean giving up our self-sufficiency, our independence. We may live for awhile in such a self-imposed bubble of "independence." But it is a fragile bubble indeed. So quickly, our self-defined independence can be shattered.

It can be shattered by many things—pain … death … separation … job loss … illness … old age … aloneness.

At such points, we discover that we are not as independent and self-sufficient as we thought. We face the reality that we share an internal rhythm that links us with each other and with our Creator. At some point, the lightning strike of reality hits us: We do need—we need others, and we need God. It is then that we come to the point where we have no other choice but to ask, "Father, give us …"

The deepest need of any man or woman is the need to overcome separateness, to leave the prison of aloneness, to find a relationship, to be cared for, and, in turn, to care. The meaning of life is not to be found in turning inward, focusing on ourselves. Joy and meaning come as we escape our island of self-centeredness and see that we do need others.

In the words of John Donne,

> No man is an island, entire of itself; every man is a
> piece of the continent, a part of the main; if a clot
> be washed away to the sea, Europe is the less … any
> man's death diminishes me, because I am involved
> in mankind; and therefore never send to know for
> whom the bell tolls; it tolls for thee.[15]

Jesus said that unless we become like children, we shall not enter the kingdom of God. Certainly many things characterize children. One characteristic that stands out, however, is their uninhibited recognition of need—and their willingness to verbalize their need:

"Hold me."

"Help me."

"I'm hungry. Can I have something to eat?"

"I'm lonely."

When we come before our heavenly Father like an uninhibited four-year-old willing to admit our needs, we are close, indeed, to the kingdom of God. As our Father, God is not the eternal vending machine, nor is he an irrelevant outsider. He is the loving father wanting the best for us.

As we grow in grace, we not only ask for our personal needs to be met, but we also pray for the needs of those about us. The Lord's Prayer does not model "give me," but "give us." Again, we are reminded that we are a part of a larger family. We are not alone. In the Christian world view, we are responsible for each other.

So we come to that time in the Lord's Prayer when we ask:

"Our Father, which art in heaven … Give us …"

… *This Day*

"Therefore I tell you, do not worry about your life, what you will eat or drink; or about your body, what you will wear … Who of you by worrying can add a single hour to his life?" (Matthew 6:25–27)

Too often, I throw away today. I am too busy fretting about what I missed yesterday or I am worrying about what I am going to confront tomorrow. In the process, I lose touch with today. I don't have time to experience this day or what it has to offer. There is too much …

anxiety

worry

frustration

exhaustion.

All too often, too much of my time and energy is spent worrying about the past and the future that I can't think about today, today. "Why did I do that yesterday? What will happen tomorrow?" I fret.

This state of mind is self-defeating, draining the joy from life. Endless fret and worry leads to inefficiency, broken relationships, and all too often, high blood pressure or peptic ulcers.

Even as I am immersed in this fog of fret and worry, I hear the voice of Jesus penetrating the confusion. "Therefore I tell you, do not be anxious about your life, what you shall eat or what you shall drink, nor about your body, what you shall put on … Your heavenly Father knows that you need them all. But seek first his kingdom and his righteousness, and all these things shall be yours as well" (Matthew 6:25, 32–33).

Jesus closes the gap between today and yesterday, today and tomorrow. He helps us see that today, after all, is all the day we have. Therefore, we should spend it wisely. If we try to live three ways at once—in worry over the mistakes of yesterday, anxious about tomorrow, and overwhelmed by today—we will be perpetually lost. Jesus helps us overcome our hurry to be some place other than where we are. He helps us focus on the wonder of today. When we have our fists clenched in anxiety and worry, we cannot extend them to receive the gifts God wants to give us today, nor can we use them to sensitively touch the world about us. Jesus helps us unclasp our anxious hands and open them to the world around us.

The Good News that Jesus brings to us is the truth that our Father in heaven himself has made it possible for us to have "life ... and have it more abundantly" (John 10:10 (KJV)). We are assured that his forgiveness covers the wrongs of the past and his Spirit energizes us to face the needs of tomorrow.

When Jesus says, "Be not afraid," he does not imply that we should ignore the future and future needs. We can and should plan and take appropriate precautions to provide for those who depend on us. However, there is a difference between planning for the future and fretting and worrying about bridges not yet crossed. I am convicted that I need to move my concerns about my basic needs and my hopes and dreams from my worry list to my prayer list. I need to be willing to trust God to guide me day by day as to how I am to use the gifts he has given me to meet the needs of today.

In our pit of worry, Jesus comes and stands by us. He says, simply, to take each day as it comes. Pray to our Father for the needs you have today. Trust him to get you through this day. Our Father wants to hear us say, "Give us today our daily bread (and whatever else we need today)."

... Our Daily Bread

Keep falsehood and lies far from me; give me neither poverty nor riches, but give me only my daily bread. Otherwise, I may have too much and disown you and say, 'Who is the Lord?' or I may become poor and steal, and so dishonor the name of my God. (Proverbs 30:8–9)

"Give us today our daily bread ..." sounds strange to most of us who take our necessities for granted. Even as we face clearly our dependency, we too often have trouble making such a simple request as this one. It is one thing to pray for the coming of the kingdom, it is another to ask for, and be thankful for, our lunch. The beauty of this petition is that we confess our dependence on God for all things, great and small. In doing so, we acknowledge that all of life is a gift. Even as we work to produce a living for ourselves and those who depend on us, we also work in partnership with God who gives us ability and opportunity to produce.

Praying this part of the Prayer brings us back to the realization that our bread, as well as the fulfillment of all our needs, ultimately comes from God. Ours is a fragile world—as disasters, natural and man-made, remind us daily. The rug of physical self-sufficiency and safety can be pulled from beneath our feet at any time. If it were not for God's grace, we would be helplessly cast upon the stormy waves of circumstance. In praying, "Give us today ..." we acknowledge that God is the source of all life and only through him are our needs ultimately met. If we pray this prayer and then simply sit down with folded hands to wait, we quite likely will starve. Food and other necessities are not going to appear ready-made in front of us. God is not going to spoon-feed us when we can feed ourselves.

Prayer and work are part of the same process. If the seed of potential given us by God is to grow, we must plant the seed, till the ground, prepare the soil, and cultivate the growth. God performs the miracle of germination, growth, and fruiting. But we must tend the growth and pick the harvest. Jesus illustrated this fact in the parable of the talents. The one servant who buried his talents, failing to invest what God had given him creatively and productively, was disowned. The ones who took what God had given them and invested it in productive effort were rewarded. Prayer is never a manipulating of God into doing for us what we can do for ourselves. True prayer is celebrating what God has done and depending on him to do what is best for us in the future.

Praying "Give us this day our daily bread ..." reminds us that opportunity and ability to work, to produce, and to master are possible only through the gift and grace of God. Praying this petition expresses our dependence on God while challenging us to use, today, the energy and abilities God has given us to be his hands in ministry to ourselves and others.

We are again reminded in the Prayer that we are a part of something larger than ourselves. Here we pray, "Give us our daily bread" not "Give me my daily bread." The plural pronoun negates all selfishness in this prayer. The natural tendency is to think of "me" and "mine" first. This essential selfishness is the first fruit of broken fellowship with the Creator and the root of so much hurt in our world. True prayer calls us out of this selfishness. When we pray this petition, by the very form of the words, we are committed to overcoming this selfishness.

How do I balance my life in a time of plenty? Am I willing to keep my wants simple and in relationship to my needs? So many people in my world do not have adequate daily bread or the essentials of life—food, housing, clothing, and medicine. What can I, one person, do to make a difference?

This petition helps me focus on the reality of my world, my dependence on God, and my responsibility to be God's hands and feet in reaching out to those around me. Those of us who are fortunate, who have our needs of the day met, who seem to be doing fine are reminded by this part of the prayer that whatever we have is a gift of God's grace. We are reminded to always be thankful.

***

Lord, I so often pray that you will keep on giving me what you have given me before when you are wanting to give me something more and different. May I have my hands open wide so that I will be ready to receive your gifts and share these gifts with others.

It is so hard for me to focus on this day. I need you to hold my hand and guide me. I must be responsible for those people and those jobs you have given me. I will need to plan and prepare. In so doing, however, let me depend on you in such a way that I am free of worry, fret, and anxiety. Your forgiveness covers my mistakes and sins of yesterday. Your grace will be sufficient for tomorrow. Your power is available today. So I go forth with you, knowing that you desire to give me what I need for today.

As I pray for my own needs, hopes, and dreams, may I not forget those who have special physical, social, and psychological needs. I pray specifically for these:

Chapter Eight
Forgive Us …

Forgive

Search me, O God, and know my heart; test me and know my anxious thoughts. See if there is any offensive way in me and lead me in the way everlasting. (Psalm 139:23)

The movie version of C. S. Lewis's story, *The Lion, the Witch and the Wardrobe* was a huge success with the public. Millions of people, young and old, saw the movie and read the books. Yet many critics gave lukewarm reviews. Although different reviewers had specific issues that they did not like, most simply did not get the central idea of the plot. The theme of the story by C. S. Lewis revolves around the failure (sin) of Edmond, one of the central characters, and the sacrificial death of Aslan the lion (the Christ figure) by which Edmond experienced forgiveness and restoration. For many of the reviewers, this was unintelligible, confusing, or outright wrong.

However, children understood. And Christians understand. Nothing, it seems, is as universal as the preoccupation with forgiveness.

Each of us, in some way, has failed. And we know it!

Deep within every human heart resides a sense of right and wrong. In our quiet moments, we know that we have failed in some way to live up to the mandate of that conscience. Inevitably, we all know guilt because we live with it. How we deal with this guilt will either drive us toward God, personal growth, and maturity or it will push us away from God and into blind alleys with no exit.

We try to hide the pain of guilt through a variety of maneuvers. Some try to escape the presence of guilt by repressing it, attempting to bury it deep in their subconscious mind. When, at unsuspecting turns in life, the guilt percolates into conscious awareness, they seek to quickly push it back below the surface by diverting their attention to something else. Others seek to numb their pain with mind-altering substances such as drugs or alcohol. Such efforts universally fail because the guilt does not go away when it is buried. It may stay hidden for a while, but repressed guilt keeps returning to haunt us. Even while buried, it is active, eating at body and soul producing emotional pain, sorrow, and, all too often, physical illness.

Then some take the opposite path. They openly caress their guilt. They dwell on it. They talk about it. It is like a heavy backpack loaded with rocks that they cannot put down. The pain is written in every line of their face. They cannot let go of their sense of imperfection and unworthiness. Their conversations are preoccupied with it. Their relationships are haunted by it.

In the end, both of these responses to guilt—repression and exhibitionism—are physically, emotionally, and spiritually destructive. Both feed the guilt, keeping it alive. One of the wonderful promises of the Christian faith is the offer of, and provision for, unconditional forgiveness which ultimately neutralizes guilt and nurtures wholeness. The words of the Prayer, "Forgive our trespasses ..." open the door to the fresh breeze of God's forgiveness and restoration. As we let God lift the burden of guilt from our shoulders, we know the joy that comes with grace—the grace of forgiving and forgetting. In this grace, our guilt is neutralized, washed away. We no longer have to fight it, hide it, or caress it.

Jesus told a poignant and lovely story about a woman caught in a cycle of desperate failure. This woman was brought to Jesus by a pious group who accused her of adultery. She was thrown in front of him by those who thought themselves worthy to punish her for her sins. Jesus, seeing deeper layers of truth, said quietly, "He that is without sin among you, let him first cast a stone at her." The scriptures state that the vengeful mob slowly drifted away.

> Jesus, looking at the woman, said, "Woman, where are they? Has no one condemned you?"
> "No one, sir," she said.
> "Then neither do I condemn you," Jesus declared. "Go and leave your life of sin." (John 8:9–11)

Whatever our failures, regardless of how far we have missed the mark, God forgives us as we bring our guilt to him. When we present our guilt to Jesus, the guilt is not buried or flouted; it is neutralized. It is washed away just as the bleach cleanses and whitens the soiled laundry. Exposed to the cleansing touch of Jesus, our guilt no longer has power over us.

This word, forgiveness, seems to be everywhere in the Bible—the aching hurts that cry for it, the longing to find it, the surprising discovery of it. The issue of forgiveness permeates so many of the personal histories recorded in the Bible. These individual stories mirror the story of human history as well as our own personal history. The Gospel story tells us that forgiveness is precisely the reason God sent his son to earth: "For God did not send his Son into the world to condemn the world, but that the world might be saved through him" (John 3:17).

Jesus does not paint God as a cosmic judge scrutinizing our lives in order to find evidence to condemn us. Rather, Jesus paints the picture of the loving father offering forgiveness. The parable of the prodigal son (or rather, the parable of the loving father) dramatically illustrates the picture of God's forgiveness. The father in this story was clearly wronged by the son who showed callous disregard for his father's love and care. Even as the son rejected the family and went defiantly on his way, the father longingly anticipated his son's return. When the father saw the wayward son trudging toward home, he ran to him "while he was still a long way off." (How many hours had this father spent gazing over the horizon for the familiar silhouette of his child?) The father hugged his repenting son, not with scorn or judgment, but with open arms and acceptance (Luke 15).

What is God like?

"The loving father with open arms!" Jesus shouts.

God holds out his forgiveness through his son as a gift. However, we must accept this gift of grace if we are to know its joy. Could it be that even those in hell are forgiven? The hell of it is that they refuse to accept that forgiveness. The Gospel of Jesus Christ is the good news of the second chance. We do not have to be prisoners of our past. In accepting God's forgiveness, we can be liberated from those compulsions and impulses that shadow us with guilt in the first place.

But God's forgiveness must be claimed. The prodigal had to return home to experience the father's love. This love was there all the time, but the son had to turn and look for it in order to see it. God's forgiveness is an integral facet of his character. It is there waiting for us. But it is not ours until we claim it. We cannot know it unless we return home. Thus we pray, "Our Father, forgive our trespasses …" This is our first step toward home.

... Our Trespasses

He does not treat us as our sins deserve or repay us according to our iniquities.
(Psalm 103:10)

Failure! Disappointment! Messed up!

If you are like me, you can say, "Been there! Done that!"

When I face myself honestly, I see imperfection, incompleteness, wrong turns, and roads of opportunity not taken. I am certain I am not the only one. Not only have we all failed and disappointed others, but we have failed and disappointed ourselves too. More important, we have disappointed God.

The Gospel has much to say to those of us who have failed, disappointed, and messed up. In the Bible, we see people, much like us, who are a mixture of success and failure, who try and fall down, who reach for the stars and stumble and fail.

Take Peter the disciple, for example. He came to Jesus' inner circle straight from his fishing boat. He was rough, loud, and unsophisticated, but he was a leader and a doer. He was apparently successful, owning his own fishing business. He knew how to get things done.

When challenged to do so, he stepped out to follow this enigmatic teacher. Jesus quickly recognized Peter's leadership qualities and obviously liked him. Soon Peter was the spokesman for the group of followers. Jesus acknowledged Peter's leadership by giving him recognition and responsibility. This is illustrated in several places in the Gospels. For example, Luke tells us that "Jesus took Peter, John and James with him and went up onto a mountain to pray" (Luke 9:28).

But Peter was far from perfect. He was impulsive and bull-headed. He overestimated his own strength and commitment. When the chips were down, he failed.

> Simon Peter asked him, "Lord, where are you going?"
> Jesus replied, "Where I am going, you cannot follow now, but you will follow later."
> Peter asked, "Lord, why can't I follow you now? I will lay down my life for you."
> Then Jesus answered, "Will you really lay down your life for me? I tell you the truth, before the rooster crows, you will disown me three times!" (John 13:36–38)

Then, it happened!

As Simon Peter stood warming himself, he was asked, "You are not one of his disciples, are you?"

He denied it, saying, "I am not."

One of the high priest's servants, a relative of the man whose ear Peter had cut off, challenged him, "Didn't I see you with him in the olive grove?" Again Peter denied it, and at that moment a rooster began to crow." (John 18:25–27)

Yes, a failure! When the chips were down, Peter folded. He had failed at a most crucial point of his life. He had not lived up to his potential or commitment.

Where does Peter go from here? What future does one have after such a failure? In the middle of his disillusionment, Peter made his decision: "I'm no use here …!"

"I am going out to fish …" (John 21:3).

But then … Peter came face to face with the Gospel of the second chance.

Early in the morning, Jesus stood on the shore, but the disciples did not realize that it was Jesus.

He called out to them, "Friends, haven't you any fish?"

… Jesus said to them, "Come and have breakfast." None of the disciples dared ask him, "Who are you?" They knew it was the Lord. Jesus came, took the bread and gave it to them, and did the same with the fish.

… When they had finished eating, Jesus said to Simon Peter, "Simon son of John, do you truly love me more than these?"

"Yes, Lord, "he said, "you know that I love you."

Jesus said, "Feed my lambs." (John 21:4, 11–15)

Yes, the Gospel of the second chance.

The Good News tells us that we are products of our past. But we are not prisoners of that past.

We do not have to be fenced in by our failures, our mistakes, our disappointments, our wrong turns, or right roads not taken. The Good News opens the door to growth and to change. We can become more than we are through the acceptance and forgiveness of Jesus Christ, the Son of God.

The Gospel of the second chance! Yes, indeed, this is the central message of the Christian faith.

... As We Forgive

Then Peter came to Jesus and asked, "Lord, how many times shall I forgive my brother when he sins against me. Up to seven times?"

Jesus answered, "I tell you, not seven times, but seventy times seven."
(Matthew 18:21–22)

"Forgive us ... as we have forgiven ..." This part of the Prayer jumps out at us, throwing us off guard. The finger is now pointing directly at us. We are called to do something.

Does this statement, "as we have forgiven," mean that we are not forgiven until we forgive? Is God's forgiveness conditional after all?

Indeed, no one is capable of taking that first step into forgiving on his own. But we do not have to take this step alone. Thankfully, Jesus is not implying that we must forgive before we experience God's grace. He is, in fact, simply stating a basic truth: We can fully know in our heart the meaning of forgiveness only as we are willing to forgive. God's forgiveness is not dependent on our forgiving, but we cannot feel, know, accept, or experience the full meaning of God's forgiveness until we respond with a forgiving heart.

True prayer confronts us with God and his forgiveness so powerfully that we are driven to forgive others. The light of God's love and forgiveness shines on us and forces us to see the ugly shadows of our unforgiving spirit. We find inner peace as we allow those dark shadows of our life to be illuminated by the light of God's love and forgiveness.

The act of granting forgiveness is a liberating experience for anyone. It frees the one doing the forgiving from anger, hurt, and the bondage of broken relationships. The willingness to forgive frees us to live again. I think Jesus is saying that we cannot enter fully into the presence of God as long as we drag along our resentments and hardness of heart.

The verb used by Jesus and translated "to forgive" originally carried the meaning "to release." To forgive is to release, to let go. "Forgive our debts" means that God has released us, freed us, from our debt of sin. Thus, when we forgive, we let go of the rope that binds us and limits our freedom of feeling and response. When we are bound by resentment and anger over past hurts, we are prisoners of these negative emotions. Jesus is saying, "Release, let go of the past, and you will be released." The very moment we "let go" and release whatever we are holding against another, we are freed to experience the positive feelings of hope, joy, and anticipation.

But I say to the Lord, "There are some things, some offenses, some people, that in my human weakness, I cannot forgive."

"Well," the Lord comes back to me, "begin where you are. Forgive when you can. Work from there. My Spirit will help you."

Forgiveness has momentum. Once we start, it is like a ball rolling downhill. It builds up force and orientation.

Again, Jesus is our mentor. One of his last prayers cried out on the cross was one of forgiveness: "Father, forgive them, for they know not what they do." He uttered these words from the cross on behalf of those who were putting him to death in the most hurtful and humiliating way. Jesus prayed as a son asking a special favor from his father—Knowing that the mercy he was asking for these men was not something they deserved, he asked nonetheless.

Jesus invites us to pray as he prayed. He invites us to experience the liberty that comes as we forgive those who have harmed or hurt us. Then we can, indeed, be free to accept and appreciate the full meaning of God's forgiveness. We can then pray, "Thank you, Father, for giving your son so that I may be forgiven. Give me the grace to forgive as I have been forgiven. Help me to release the pent-up hurt, anger, and hatred hiding in my soul."

Keep on Growing

But grow in the grace and knowledge of our Lord and Savior Jesus Christ. To him be glory both now and forever. (2 Peter 3:18)

The sixteen high school girls were lined up on the stage. Their fresh smiles hid the busy week of hard work. This night was the final session of the state Junior Miss competition, and their long hours of practice had prepared them well for it. We were attending because we had hosted two of the girls in our home for the week.

Throughout the evening, there had been singing and dancing, and it was now time for each girl to give a two-minute speech on a subject important to her.

One of the girls, a strong contender in the overall competition, spoke on the subject of family. She told of the struggle her family went through during the past year following the sudden death of a close relative. "In the face of this tragedy," she said, "we decided that we were not going to give up. We decided that we were not going to just go on living. Instead, we decided to grow."

As the rest of the program rushed past me, I could not get her words out of my mind. *"Instead, we decided to grow."* Her words challenged me and made me think more pointedly about my Christian walk.

Growing is what we are about as Christians. Many of us will be confronted sooner or later by tragedy. Most will at some point face stomach-wrenching anxiety. All of us will experience loss, hurt, and disappointment along the course of our lives. We will at some point fail. We will hurt those we love—and likely many we don't even know.

Such painful life events can "break" us or "make" us. The results depend on how we respond to these inevitable pebbles and boulders strewn in our life path. We can cave in, give up, or just fade away. We can be frayed and torn by resentment. We can just simply go on "getting by" until we die. Or we can grow.

The day after the Junior Miss competition, I was leading a Bible study for young adults. We were studying Psalm 51, David's prayer at the moment he was confronted with his guilt over the affair with Bathsheba.

In this Psalm, David pours out his painful confession to God and pleads for God's salvation and mercy. He then chooses to grow—stretched by God's forgiveness and challenge. He writes:

> Restore to me the joy of your salvation, and grant
> me a willing spirit to sustain me. Then I will teach
> transgressors your ways, and sinners will turn back to
> you.
> O Lord, open my lips, and my mouth will declare
> your praise. (Psalm 51:12–14)

David did not escape the consequences of his sins against God and the harm he brought to others but he was released from the guilt of it. He then could grow as a servant of God and as a minister to his people.

Paul and Silas were jailed in Philippi for speaking of Jesus. This interruption to their lives occurred at the moment their work was taking on accelerating momentum. It had to be a great disappointment as well as a personal hardship to be throttled at this crucial time in their ministry. They could easily have given up. But they chose to grow in grace and boldness. The writer of the book of Acts tells what happened:

> After they had been severely flogged, they were
> thrown into prison and the jailer was commanded
> to guard them carefully. Upon receiving such orders,
> he put them in the inner cell and fastened their feet
> to the stocks. About midnight Paul and Silas were

praying and singing hymns to God, and the other
prisoners were listening to them. (Acts 16:23–25)

We know what happened next. God visited that place. And based on the
joy and optimism exhibited by Paul and Silas, many came to believe in the
power and grace of God that night.

Paul continued his work as a tentmaker and a missionary. His life was
marked by accomplishment, meaningful relationships, joys, sorrows, and
some disappointments. But he continued to grow. Much later, we find him
again a prisoner, now in Rome. The temptation to pull back or give in must
have been great. He certainly could be tempted to just "get by." But, no, he
chose to keep on growing. He shares with us his personal challenge to grow:

> Not that I have already obtained all this, or have
> already been made perfect, but I press on to take
> hold of that for which Christ Jesus took hold of me.
> Brothers, I do not consider myself yet to have taken
> hold of it. But one thing I do: Forgetting what is
> behind and straining toward what is ahead, I press on
> toward the goal to win the prize for which God has
> called me heavenward in Christ Jesus.
> (Philippians 3:12–14)

Paul stands as an example to us as a person who lived life to its fullest. He
kept on growing to the very end.

A while back, my son pointed out to me a truth he had learned. He said,
"Guilt looks back; anxiety looks around; faith looks ahead." God calls us to
look ahead and to grow. As we do, he also gives us the strength to overcome
our guilt and anxieties.

Yes, I am thankful to the young junior miss, mature beyond her teen
years, for reminding me to look ahead. As God's child, I am called not to cave
in, not to just go on, but to grow—to become what God is creating me to be.
Praying, "Forgive us our trespasses" is a first step on the journey to growth.

***

*Father, you are calling us to openly confess our frail humanity and to know
the forgiveness and empowering grace of your son. May we take the step of honest
confession and acceptance of your gift of grace. Help us to accept your forgiveness*

and to grow past resentment, hurt, and self-centeredness. Help us to release the pent-up hurt, anger, and hatred hiding in our souls.

Chapter Nine
Lead Us Not into Temptation

Lead Us Not Into ...

Watch and pray so that you will not fall into temptation. The spirit is willing but the flesh is weak. (Matthew 26:41)

To live is to choose. Each person makes many major and minor choices every day. It is through this choosing that each of us traces out the trail of our own life. The Bible teaches that this innate capacity to make choices was planted in each person by God. It all began with Adam and Eve.

As these, our first ancestors, illustrated, we can choose between alternatives ...

left or right
better or best
right or wrong
obedience or rebellion
good or evil.

Temptation is the force, the pull, to make choices that are not in tune with our design or the will of our Creator. Each person, from personal experience, knows such temptation in a very real way. Every day, we hear a cacophony of voices calling us in many different directions, some good, some bad. We must choose which of these voices we will follow and which ones we will resist. The freedom of choice means we can make a right choice or a wrong choice. And as it was with Adam and Eve, we are drawn to the attractive, to the expedient, to the shortest route to having our needs met or getting what we want.

Indeed, to live is to choose!

Most of the time, temptation calls us to commit acts of hurt, deception, or unfaithfulness—to act deliberately in a wrong way. Everyone, at some time or another, experiences the impulse to perform such deliberate acts of wrongdoing. At times, we resist, even defeat, the impulse. At other times, we do give in and then feel guilty about our wrong choices and wrong acts.

While most of us may recognize the impulse to do wrong through deliberate acts, we easily fall prey to the more insidious temptation. This is the pull to not act, the temptation not to do good when we could. The inclination to not act is the sin that Jesus seemed to despise the most. In the parable of the Good Samaritan, the robbers who hurt and stole from the victim were guilty of sin. However, the Levite and scribe who chose to walk around the victim ignoring his needs were also guilty. Indeed, as we look at our own hearts, we recognize that we are much more vulnerable to the sin of omission—the sin of not acting when action is called for.

Jesus knew about all these temptations his followers would face. As the Son of God, as Creator, he knew the human design and all the details of human nature. He knew just how free our free will is. As the Son of Man, however, he lived in this world, experiencing personally all the challenges of human existence. He was bombarded by temptation in a dramatic way in the wilderness of Judea at the beginning of his ministry. Temptation, however, continued to haunt him daily as he was confronted with the worst and the best that human life had to offer. As the writer of Hebrews reminds us, "For we do not have a high priest who is unable to sympathize with our weaknesses, but we have one who has been tempted in every way, just as we have ..." (Hebrews 4:15).

In the gripping, terse account of the temptations of Jesus as narrated in the Gospels, we sense the presence of powerful forces pulling on his humanity. During that time alone in the wilderness, he was relentlessly pursued. He was surely hearing the same chorus of voices that call to us. Jesus' choices, however, were epic in their ramifications. Would he choose the way of God, his Father, or the way of power and expediency urged by the tempter? His choice would determine whether he was to walk in God's way or to take his own shortcuts.

Jesus saw through the deception of the tempter because he was grounded in God's will. He was fortified by his knowledge of the revealed Word of God and his daily communion with the Father. He fended off each of the devil's assaults with scripture that countered the devil's propositions. Jesus faced openly the powerfully attractive temptations thrown at him and made the choice to follow God's plan whatever the consequences.

This example of Jesus challenges us to face temptation confidently for we know that he has walked where we walk. He has been tempted in all ways as we have. Thus, as we pray the petition, "Lead us not into temptation," we acknowledge that we cannot deal with temptation by ourselves. We admit that we need a power which is not our own in order to emerge triumphant from the test and make the right choices.

Jesus understands, better than we do, the power temptation holds over us. In his prayer for his followers expressed in John 17:15, Jesus anticipated the human situation: "My prayer is not that you take them out of the world but that you protect them from the evil one." Jesus is not asking that his followers escape temptation. Rather he prays that they will have victory over temptation. He is not praying for exemption from temptation for his followers but the conquest of temptation in their lives. Thus as we pray, "Lead us not into temptation …," we are acknowledging that we live in a sea of temptation—It surrounds us, for there cannot be life without it. But when temptation does come, we pray that God will give us strength to face it and make the right choices.

Thus the petition, "Lead us not into temptation," is the honest prayer of the man or woman who knows how true Jesus' words are: "The spirit is willing but the flesh is weak." It is a petition of one who recognizes how dangerous this world is, how thoroughly the forces of evil are marshaled, and how weak and vulnerable he or she is in the face of abounding evil. It is a humble call to the Father for help in facing the choices of this day.

Temptation is unrelenting. It is always stalking us. We must deal with it daily. Just as we have been encouraged to pray for our "daily bread," we need to pray daily for the energy and resolve to resist the devil and his temptations. We need to remember daily how vulnerable we are. Daily, we need to pray, "Lead us not into temptation …"

Who Am I?

"Which of these three do you think was a neighbor to the man who fell into the hands of the robbers?" (Luke 10:36)

As I flip through the pages of the newspaper, I am struck by how frequently news means "something bad is happening to someone." Headlines blare out disconcerting messages: Storm leaves hundreds of thousands dead; Two men murdered last night in the city; Three children found abused and abandoned; Drug abuse up among latchkey children … The list goes on.

Occasionally, there is a headline about something good happening but such good news seems pretty rare.

Most of the time, I read these headlines, scan the stories, and nonchalantly flip to the next page. I am secretly thankful that all this bad news seems to be far away from my comfortable sofa at home.

Then in my quiet time, I open my Bible to Luke 10 and the familiar story of the Good Samaritan. As I read, a sense of uneasiness pricks at my sense of safety and self-satisfaction.

The words rivet my attention. "A man was going down from Jerusalem to Jericho, when …"

Most everyone knows this story by heart. In a few succinct words, Jesus draws distinct portraits of four different groups of people.

There is a victim. The victim is a person whose life has been shattered by circumstances. He is hurt; his life is interrupted. "I am simply going about my business," this unsuspecting victim would say.

There are those who hurt. In the guise of the robbers who attacked the traveler, we see those whose ability to love and care has been warped and shrunk. Their motto is, "Me first. Get what you can. Kill if you must." Their natural human instincts for relationship have been crippled. They have lost their sense of responsiveness and responsibility to their fellow human beings. Unfortunately, this warped sense of life has been all too prevalent in the human family from the beginning. Controlled to some degree by society, this attitude of hate and hurt is not far below the surface and will spring up when least expected.

There are the bystanders. Their motto is, "Live and let live." They exist in their own "independent" world, too preoccupied to think and feel beyond their own needs. They closely guard their expense of time, energy, and emotional commitment. They have no intention of deliberately hurting or taking from another. But they seldom go out of their way to help. Like the priest and Levite in the story, they walk on the other side when possible.

Such bystanders draw a circle around their commitments. They will reach out to those inside their circle: family, friends, tribe members, and maybe those who they think can help them. But they jealously guard the range of their commitments. They are simply too occupied with their own "urgencies" to notice.

There are the helpers. The one we call the Good Samaritan exemplifies a very different attitude. He lived the motto, "Live and help live."

The Good Samaritan and those like him recognize their interdependence. They know they are part of, and belong to, a community; they are a part of something larger than themselves. They reach out beyond their own limited circle of self-interest to touch others and give into the community about them. They are free emotionally to respond to that "neighbor" near them. They live in an "open range" with no fences to hem in their roaming, spontaneous spirits.

Looking into my own heart, I find that all of these characters live there.

A part of me is selfish and hurting and would be like the robbers if I were bold enough. That secret side of me whispers, "Live for yourself; do your own thing, whatever it costs."

For me, the loudest voice is the one that says, "Live and let live. I'll take care of myself. Let the other guy take care of his own problems. His needs are not my business." Fortunately, most of us are inhibited by our conscience from becoming brutes—killing, hurting, and maiming without cause. We are, however, sorely tempted to stand by, looking in the other direction as long as we and ours are not threatened. At least I know that for me, it is easy to walk on the other side of the road.

It is natural for us to become incensed at the robbers or anyone like them perpetuating pain—the charlatan who takes advantage of the tsunami victims, the parent who abandons and injuries his child, the abortion provider, the slum landlord. Such sins of commission bring out the passion in us. As we discussed earlier, Jesus seemed much more concerned about sins of omission than those of commission. It seems the dishonest tax collector, the adulterous woman, and the forceful Roman soldier were more responsive to Jesus' outreach than the pious and self-satisfied who wrapped themselves in smugness while being oblivious to obvious needs about them.

The picture Jesus paints of the last judgment in Matthew 25 is haunting: "He will reply, 'I tell you the truth, whatever you did not do for one of the least of these, you did not do for me'" (Matthew 25:39). Those left out of the kingdom at the end are not left out because of what they did; they are left out for what they did not do.

As we listen to Jesus, our consciences will not easily let us get by with a sideline walk. Deep down inside—in our quieter moments when we are alone with ourselves, in our dreams—we wince at the bystander side of ourselves.

Then there are times when I feel deep within my soul a tinge of the Good Samaritan and his spirit which says, "Live and help live." The voice is often faint and weak, but it is there. That voice calls me to grow and go beyond my intimate, selfish circle and share with those out there—in the marketplace, the office, the factory, the school, the field, the warehouse.

At the end of the parable, Jesus reflected the original question back to the one who asked, "Who is my neighbor?" with a slight twist. Jesus asked him, "Who is the neighbor to him who fell among the thieves?"

Today, Jesus is asking each of us, "Whose neighbor are you?" He is challenging us to grow into the kind of person who can act with the same motives as the Good Samaritan. Only when we see ourselves as we really are can we grow toward the character God wants us to be.

So we pray for protection from temptation knowing we are most susceptible to the call "not to do." As we pray, the words of Jesus ring loudly in our ears: "Go and do likewise."

Deliver Us from Evil

"The spirit is willing, but the body is weak". (Mark 14:38)

The Bible teaches that evil is more than a nebulous, fleeting concept, a philosophy, a thought, or an ethical construct. Evil, in the form of the Evil One, is alive and moving about creation, ever stalking the created. The Bible frequently reminds us of the personal nature of evil. This Evil One, disguised as enticing and adventuresome, accosted Eve in the garden. He captured her attention and swayed her choices. Later in the Bible story, we see the dramatic picture of this Evil One strutting about, plotting against Job. This word picture of personified evil is one of the most vivid images in all literature. Then in the boldest move ever, Evil, in the form of Satan, confronted Jesus at his most vulnerable moments, tempting him to ignore God's plan and improvise his own. All of these encounters dramatically illustrate that evil is ever present, actively looking for our vulnerable points.

The Evil One confronts each of us when we least expect it with the promise of an easier way, maybe a more exciting way, to reach our goals. Always in the shadows of our lives, we hear his steps; we feel his hot breath on our necks. He comes, however, not as a grotesque monster with pitchfork in hand but as a friendly acquaintance offering enticing choices which seem innocent and stimulating.

Thus, the great battle between good and evil encircles all of us. The battleground on which this war rages is our human heart. Paul vividly describes this battle in Romans 7: "When I want to do good, evil is right there with me." All of us, in one way or another, know that Paul is speaking for us. I know I identify with Paul for I feel the battle in my heart. I know evil is around me; I know I am vulnerable.

Thankfully, Paul does not end on this fateful note. He goes on to say, "Who will rescue me from this body of death? Thanks be to God, through Jesus Christ our Lord!" (Romans 7:21–25). We do not have to cower fearfully in the face of the Evil One. We have with us the same power that Jesus had when he faced off with Satan. We may be scorched by the heat, but we have the promise that God is with us. If we call upon him, God will give us the eyes to see evil for what, and who, it is and he will give us the strength to confront it. Thus Jesus teaches us to pray, "Lead us not into temptation but deliver us from the evil one."

One of the great promises of the scriptures is that we are not alone in the battle. Amy Carmichael, who as a missionary to India saw evil up close in the desperate poverty of body and spirit of the people she served, reassures us, "But we were not meant to live on a perpetual stormy sea. We are meant to pass through and find harbor and so be at peace. Then we are free from occupation with ourselves and our storm—we are free to help others."[16]

***

Lord, I know that I cannot stand up to the Evil One in my own strength. I need you. Do deliver me from the Evil One. Give me the wisdom to see temptation as it is, even when dressed in sheep's clothing. Give me the strength to resist when I see it. Give me the desire for victory over it.

Temptations are so subtle. They come quietly; they attack always at my point of weakness. When I am tempted to take shortcuts, help me to stand firm as you did.

Chapter Ten
For Thine Is the Kingdom and the Power and the Glory

For Thine Is ...

*And my God will meet all your needs according to his glorious riches in Christ Jesus."(*Philippians 4:19)

"For thine is the kingdom and the power and the glory ..."

For several reasons, many biblical scholars believe these words, forming the last sentence of the Prayer in the Authorized Version, were not part of the original prayer as given by Jesus. This conclusion is based on the fact that this epilogue is not found in all the early manuscripts. It is possible, some scholars propose, that these words became part of the Lord's Prayer as a natural response by the early congregations to the words of Jesus. In time, this response became so much a part of the oral tradition that it was appropriately appended as commentary to the end of the recorded prayer. I certainly don't know how these beautiful closing words came to be part of the Prayer as we know it. I do know that these words speak the longings of my heart as I come to the end of the Prayer.

Whatever the means by which it happened, this lovely doxology did find its way into many manuscripts. Early in the history of the church, it became an intimate part of the Prayer. It has continued to speak to worshipers, both individually and corporately, through the ages. "For thine is ..." accentuates the central theme of the Prayer. It acknowledges the centrality of God in all things. It reaffirms God as ultimate power—but also ultimate good. As we honestly say these words at the end of the Prayer, we affirm that we are submitting to God's will and power now, where we are, this day.

"For thine is ..." acknowledges and reinforces the central truth of the Lord's Prayer. It reinforces the awareness that God is creator, owner, sustainer, and giver. Everything, from the myriad of galaxies spinning in space to the simple joy in the human heart when two friends meet, is all a gift from God, the Loving Father of the Lord's Prayer. So we respond to this, as we should respond to all prayer, with the submission of a child to his or her Father.

"For thine is the glory ..." reminds us of two things: It reminds us to whom we are praying, and it reminds us that we are praying to the One who was here at the beginning and who will be here at the end of all that is. These words express the sense of awe and humility that should permeate all honest worship.

The Kingdom and the Power and the Glory Forever

To him who is able to keep you from falling and to present you before his glorious presence without fault and with great joy—to the only God our Savior be glory, majesty, power and authority, through Jesus Christ our Lord, before all ages, now and forevermore. Amen. (Jude 1:24)

This doxology at the end of the Prayer with its beautiful simplicity reminds us of the central, eternal truths of the Gospel:

Thine is the kingdom. We are reminded that God is in charge of all that we see, feel, and hear with our senses as well as all that is beyond our perception. The Prayer ends with the recognition that God is the cosmic monarch. We are his subjects. By pledging obedience and allegiance to him, we find our rightful place in life and the world—and ultimately in heaven.

Thine is the power. The Greek word translated into English as "power" is derived from the same root as "dynamite." We thus end the Prayer by acknowledging the creative and sustaining energy of God. We come to the end thinking of the God who loves us like a father but who has the power to speak into existence all that is and who has the power to bring it all to an end when he chooses. We end our prayer in the confidence that, in his love, God has heard and that he has the power to act in our best interests.

Thine is the glory. Throughout his ministry, Jesus pounded home to his followers the truth that God is our Father. We are his children. We are his creation. But we must not forget, in this intimacy, that God is transcendent. He is far above and beyond our capability of understanding him. With these words, we remind ourselves that we are in the presence of divine glory. We come into his presence with awe, excitement, and yes, even a hint of fear. Indeed, the ground about him is holy. We must take off our shoes. We are the closest to eternity when we sing from the heart, "Glory to God in the highest."

In response to this kingdom of power and glory, let us come to prayer always with fresh anticipation and devout humility. "So begins a communion, a talking with God, a coming-to-one with Him, which is the end of prayer, yea, of existence itself."[17]

Through prayer, all honest prayer, the fresh breeze of heaven blows on us. Frank Laubach, the missionary and educator of the last century, adds, "And I add another resolve—to be as wide open toward people and their need as I am toward God. Windows open outward as well as upward! … Open your soul and entertain the glory of God and after a while that glory will be reflected in the world about you and in the very clouds above your head."[18]

May we all keep the windows to our soul open to God and to others.

Amen

May the words of my mouth and the meditation of my heart be pleasing in your sight, O Lord, my Rock and myRedeemer. (Psalm 19:14)

Men and women of faith have long appended the "Amen" to their prayers. "Amen" is an expression with origins deep in both the Hebrew and Greek language and culture. The root meaning of the word, amen, is "true," or "faithful." A literal translation is something like, "So be it!" From long ago, amen has been used to confirm and affirm a statement, belief, or commitment.

It was the custom, passed on from the synagogues into the early Christian assemblies, when one had read or offered up a solemn prayer to God, the other believers in attendance responded with "Amen." They thus claimed the substance of what was uttered as their own.

Justin (sometimes called Justin Martyr) who lived from about AD 100–165 gives us a vivid picture of this custom as practiced in the early church. Justin was a well-educated pagan born in Samaria. After studying many philosophies and religions, he became a Christian. Being well read and educated, he spoke forcefully in defense of the faith, even writing a detailed essay to the emperor summarizing the key points of the Christian faith which has been preserved as the *First Apology* of Justin. He was eventually martyred for his commitment to the Way of Christ.

Justin gives us a window into the worship of the early Christians:

> At the end of prayers, we greet one another with a kiss. Then the president of the brethren brings bread and a cup of wine mixed with water; and he takes them, and offers up praise and glory to the Father of the universe, through the name of the Son and of the Holy Ghost, and gives thanks at considerable length for our being counted worthy to receive these things at his hands. When he has concluded the prayers and thanksgiving, all of the people present express their joyful assent by saying "Amen" ("Amen" means "so be it" in Hebrew) ... Then those whom we call deacons give to each of those present the bread and wine mixed with water over which the thanksgiving was pronounced and carry away a portion to those who are absent.[19]

As we can see, affirming prayer with "Amen" was a custom of great importance in the early church. Most of us are intimately familiar with the use of amen in contemporary Christian practice. Unfortunately, we all too easily offer the amen perfunctorily, even carelessly, without thought of its implication. However, our amen contains great and magnificent implications; it carries profound import for all of us as supplicants. By the very nature of its meaning, the amen calls us to pause, letting the significance of the words we have prayed sink deep into our being. Let us take seriously the commitment implied in this simple statement. When we affix the amen to our prayers, we are saying, "Lord, I really mean this. I really want this to happen. I commit myself to it." Thus, at the end of the Lord's Prayer, we sense an overwhelming need to call out with our heart and voice, "Amen." In so doing, we are saying,

"Yes!"

"So be it."

"Let it happen!"

Thus having prayed the Lord's Prayer—the model prayer, the Disciples' Prayer—we rise from our knees and go into the world reverent, humble, awed by God's sovereignty. We pledge our obedience to him, remembering the intimacy of "Our Father" and the infiniteness of his power. We trust in that intimacy and that power to sustain us. And in response, we confess our amen.

***

Lord, I come to you acknowledging that I need you. You create and you sustain all that is. Let me not forget that in all times and all places you are in charge. May I open my eyes and see your beauty, your strength, and your love.

Lord, I am not always sincere with my "Amen." Often, the nearest I can come is wanting to want to. Today, Lord, I want to want to say "Amen" to the Lord's Prayer, "Amen" to your power and glory—with all of its implications and possibilities. May I plant the words in my heart this day.

Chapter Eleven
Epilogue
Steps along the Journey of Prayer

This Too Will Pass

And we know that in all things God works for the good of those who love him, who have been called according to his purpose. (Romans 8:28)

A while back, I had lunch with a friend who was going through a particularly difficult time in his life. Not only had he experienced the death of a close relative, but he was facing tough decisions about work.

"The stress itself is painful," he said. "But the real pain comes from the fact that I cannot feel God's presence right now." He paused to take another bite of lunch. "As a Christian, I know in my head that God loves and cares for me. But the fact is, I do not feel it right now."

Our perception of God's presence is certainly affected by many factors.

At times, circumstances seem to gang up on us. We are so overwhelmed by pain, loss, or conflict brought on by the circumstances that we are numbed—even to God's presence. At other times, we are so caught up in the hustle of the urgencies in our life that we do not pause long enough to sense God's presence.

Often, however, our awareness of God is controlled by our inner mood cycles. Indeed, our emotional state affects our spiritual sensitivities as we go from spiritual monsoons to dry deserts. The tone of our entire life is flavored by these fluctuating moods. Most, if not all, men and women have mood cycles alternating from periods of well-being, energy, and initiative to periods of depression and dissatisfaction. During these times, we are less able to cope with the frustrations of life, to make decisions, and to experience peace. Our spiritual relationships—with God and with others—are disrupted. On the other hand, during the other end of the cycle, the high times in our lives, we are more likely to have a sense of confidence and joy. We feel extra close to God and others.

A friend of mine who had been active in ministry became depressed. He withdrew from activities he once was enthusiastic about and was not able to enjoy the fellowship of his friends. He no longer liked church and felt distant from God. "God seems so far away and so unreal to me anymore," he said. Just about every believer has experienced such dry spells in his or her spiritual journey. When we are lost in such a spiritual desert, we are less capable of experiencing meaning, hope, or happiness.

"There was a time when I was anxious, even frightened, by the spiritual deserts in my life," I told my friend. "But I have come to accept them as a part of the scenery along my spiritual journey."

I was particularly helped by an anecdote related by President Abraham Lincoln facing the threat of Civil War. He told the story of an Eastern monarch who instructed his wise men to come up with a statement that would be appropriate in all situations. After some deliberation, they presented him with these words: "And this, too, shall pass away."

Lincoln marveled at this simple wisdom. "How chastening in an hour of pride. How consoling in an hour of stress and affliction," he reflected. He noted that these are words we need to hear when we are at the peak of success and when we are in the depths of failure.

My own experience has shown me the truth of these words, and they have helped me deal with the ups and downs of my own spiritual life. When it comes to my feelings and emotions, nothing is constant. Nothing stays the same. But God is the same. His presence is constant even when I do not feel it. I have learned that if I will stay open to God when I am in the desert, he will open to me a spiritual oasis where I can drink the cool water of his love and presence. Knowing this, I can press on even in the middle of the desert, knowing that "This, too, will pass."

The years have taught me that certain things will help me stay open to God even when I do not "feel" his presence.

I must tell myself that God's presence is not dependant on my feelings. I can know from previous experience and the revelation of the Bible, as well as the testimonies of those who have gone before me, that God is most present when he is least visible.

I can listen to what the scriptures say about God and his love:

"Weeping may remain for a night but rejoicing comes in the morning" (Psalm 30:5).

"But I tell you the truth: It is for your good that I am going away. Unless I go away, the Counselor will not come to you ..." (John 16:7).

In a little while, you will see me no more, and then after a little while you will see me (John 16:16).

"Praise be to the God and Father of our Lord Jesus Christ, the Father of compassion and the God of all comfort, who comforts us in all our troubles, so that we can comfort ... (2 Corinthians 2:3–4).

I can practice the presence of God every day by setting aside time to focus on him whether I feel his presence then or not. I do this by reading scriptures, particularly those with a promise. I read what the other Christians say about their relationship with God. I pray. I can always pray the Lord's Prayer with its direct claim of God as our Father. The Lord's Prayer is an instructive and affirming companion during these times of drought.

I can focus on others. When we are blue, unhappy, or anxious, the worst thing we can do is to focus inwardly, fretting over our situation and our negative feelings. The more we focus on ourselves, the more depressed we are likely to become. We must look up and out to the world around us. As we get involved in meeting others' needs, we are more likely to forget our own. As we get involved in meeting the needs of others and the needs of the community as a whole, we find God close by.

Once, when I was in a particularly unhappy point in my life, I visited the dentist. As I pushed back in the chair, my eyes rested on a poster attached to the ceiling. The words shot right through my self-preoccupation: "Happiness is like a butterfly. Chase it and it will fly away from you. Get busy in other things and before you know it, it will come and rest on your shoulder."

Yes, when it comes to my feelings and emotions, nothing is constant. Nothing stays the same. But God is the same. God's presence is constant even when I do not feel it. If I am open to God, he will find me. In the times of famine, I try to remember the words of a former pastor who said, "Sometimes God calms the storm. Sometimes he lets the storm rage but he calms the heart of his child."

Stepping Out on the Journey of Prayer

"Lord, teach us to pray ... " (Luke 11:1)

Thus, I write this book not because I am accomplished in prayer. I do not speak as one who has arrived at the destination. I too often find myself traveling through spiritual deserts seeking the moisture of God's Spirit. I speak only as a fellow traveler on the journey of prayer who is struggling to overcome his own spiritual anemia. I struggle to experience prayer and all of its meaning more deeply. On this journey of discovery, the Lord's Prayer has been a stimulating companion and teacher. While it comforts when I need comforting, it also prods me to keep moving, keep learning, keep seeking, and keep growing.

Even as I sense more than ever my need for prayer, I must continue to work at putting my good intentions into action. In the push and pull of everyday life, I, and most other people I know, have trouble finding time to pray, or more important, a time to pray. We make some effort at praying but find that we do not sustain the effort because of the pressures of daily living. Frustrated, we easily give up the continuing pursuit. Prayer then, too easily, becomes primarily an "emergency flare" sent up when we face a crisis or sense a personal need. Unfortunately, if we never grow beyond this concept of prayer, we miss out on the best that our Creator has for us.

As we have seen, prayer as Jesus modeled it, is much more than an emergency flare or personal crutch in time of injury. To Jesus, prayer was natural and vital. It was alive and relevant to his daily living. As we catch this spirit of prayer from Jesus, our prayer becomes a priority in our day-to-day living—not just an episodic emergency resource kit. If prayer is to be real to us as it was to Jesus, we must choose for prayer to be a central part of our lives. At first, we may feel we do not know how to find a time or a place for prayer. We don't even know how to begin. But if we will let him, Jesus will show us the way. By the example of his own prayer life, he models several ways to experience meaningful prayer.

Pray regularly. Throughout the Gospels, we see Jesus praying routinely. We read in Mark, "Very early in the morning, while it was still dark, Jesus got up, left the house and went off to a solitary place, where he prayed" (Mark 1:35).

The more prayer becomes a part of our daily lives, as essential as eating, the more we know its power. For the pressured and busy people of today's rapidly paced world, finding the time to pray seems hard, if not impossible. The only solution is to just start. This first effort may be a quick minute in the morning while drinking our orange juice; it may be a quiet moment after lunch at work; it may be a minute or two before going to bed at night. Whatever the time, one simply stops all other activity and focuses on God. The testimony of many is that once begun, these moments are so meaningful that one earnestly seeks to expand the time set aside to meet God.

Pray in depth. Prayer can penetrate even more deeply into our souls when we turn away from the pressures of life for a longer period of in-depth reflection and prayer. A good first step would be to set aside a little more time for extended prayer and mediation at least weekly. This, then, becomes a regular appointment with God. For some, time on a weekend may be best. For others, it may be lunch one day a week. Each of us will have to discover the best time for us.

Jesus was as busy as any of us (and his work was certainly important). Yet, he made time for retreat with extended time for prayer and reflection. Luke tells us, for example, that during a very active time of his ministry, Jesus took his trusted friends and "went up onto a mountain to pray" (Luke 9:28).

Pray spontaneously. Certainly meaningful prayer does not have to be planned or staged. Paul enjoins us: "Be joyful always; pray continually; give thanks in all circumstances, for this is God's will for you in Christ Jesus" (1 Thessalonians 5:18). He is simply accentuating a common theme seen in Jesus' life. Throughout the Gospels, we see Jesus repeatedly stopping during his day to pray for something or someone who appeared in his path. Each day presents us with myriads of opportunities to pray. We face circumstances in work or relationships where we know we need help. We feel the wrenching of anxiety in our gut as we must perform a difficult task, or we meet someone with an acute, urgent need. At such moments, we gain assurance and strength as we utter a sentence prayer, even the Lord's Prayer. We think of someone who has a need and we pray as we drive. We get a phone call from a long-lost friend or our mate. We utter a prayer of thanksgiving for them. We see a magnificent sunset or a beautiful flower, or we hear a moving piece of music, or we read of a special need in the newspaper. In all of these situations, we can pray right there—wherever, whenever, whatever the circumstances. These spontaneous moments of prayer remind us that God is here in our world, that he is above and beyond the creation and yet involved in it.

Jump-Starting Prayer

We do not know what we ought to pray for, but the Spirit himself intercedes for us ... (Romans 8:26).

Bishop N. T. Wright[20] suggests three ways the Lord's Prayer can help us jump-start our prayer journey even when we are stalled without a clue as to how we can talk to God.

To begin with, the Prayer can provide a framework for our daily prayer and devotion. In this process, we take each phrase of the Prayer sequentially. As we dwell on the individual phrases, we voice our related hopes, dreams, and requests. For instance, when we pray, "Thy kingdom come," we can pray for peace—in the world, in our church, in our family. When we pray, "Give us our daily bread," we can pray for specific physical needs—our own or those of others. We go though the Prayer one step at a time, hanging on each phrase what is on our heart.

At another time, we might choose to let the Lord's Prayer speak for our deep-felt longings. We pray through the whole prayer slowly, reflecting on the words and in the process seek to feel God's presence. We let the words of the Prayer permeate our minds, souls, and bodies as we speak them slowly and deliberately. This method can be comforting and refreshing at times of deep need or stress. At such moments, the Prayer, in a very real way, speaks for us.

Some might choose to let the Prayer be a platform for deep meditation. In this method, one takes one phrase of the prayer each day, dwells on that phrase, and keeps meditating on it during his or her quiet time and maybe throughout the whole day. For example, on Monday, it can be, "Our Father which art in heaven." On Tuesday, it would be, "Hallowed be thy name." And thus proceed through the week.

One of these techniques will appeal to some. Others will find all three useful. Some will not like any of them. The Prayer is yours to experience in whatever way works for you. Experiment. See what is right for you. I don't think God particularly cares how you say your words. More than anything else, he just wants to hear your voice and feel your spirit.

We Are All on a Journey

Early on in this book, I wrote that I do not share these reflections because I have arrived at the ultimate destination of prayer. I write as a testimony to the longing I share with so many others to know the ultimate meaning of life. Now, many years later and many miles down the road from the time and place when and where I met John and diagnosed his anemia, I find that for me, spiritual nurture is an ever-present and ongoing need. I know now from experience that there is no one-time fix for the spiritual hunger that pushes me toward God. I know more than ever that I need to meet God daily. I have come to see the reality of Oswald Chambers' statement, "Prayer does not fit us for the greater works; prayer is the greater work."[21] Only as I am nurtured by God's continued presence will I be all that I can be.

I have learned that the important thing is that we begin to pray, that we start somewhere and keep at it. And when we don't know any other way to begin, we can always begin with the prayer that Jesus taught us:

Our Father which art in heaven, hallowed be thy name.
Thy kingdom come. Thy will be done on earth, as it is in heaven.
Give us this day our daily bread
And forgive us our debts as we forgive our debtors.
And lead us not into temptation but deliver us from evil.
For thine is the kingdom and the power and the glory forever.

Amen.

***

Lord, help me to know that you are here—in this world where we are—even in those times when I do not feel your presence. Help me to know that your love for me is not dependent on my feelings about you.
As I complete this time of intense reflection on the Lord's Prayer, may I not escape the grasp of these powerful words. May I in my daily walk seek to live out the imperatives of every thought expressed in the Prayer.

And now finally, let us pray!

Be ...
Be still ...
Be still and know ...
Be still and know that I am God.

Psalm 46:10

Notes:

1   William James, *Principles of Psychology*, in *Great Books of the Western World* Volume 53 (Chicago: Encyclopedia Britannica, 1952) p. 203.

2   Augustine, *Confessions* (Penguin, 1961) p. 21.

3   George McDonald, *Creation in Christ* (Wheaton, IL: Harold Shaw, 1976) p. 312.

4   Paul Tournier, *The Meaning of Persons* (New York: Harper and Row, 1957) p. 163.

5   Evelyn Underhill, *The Spiritual Life* (Harrisburg, PA: Morehouse Publishing, 1937) p. 55.

6   Brother Lawrence, *The Practice of the Presence of God* (Springdale, PA: Whitaker House, 1982) p. 29.

7   C. S. Lewis, *The World's Last Night and Other Essays* (New York: Harcourt Brace Jovanovich, 1963) p. 8.

8   C. S. Lewis, *Mere Christianity* (New York: Macmillan, 1958) p. 36.

9   Frank Laubach, *Frank, Letters by a Modern Mystic* (Westwood, NJ: Fleming Revell, 1937) p. 61.

10 Eugene Peterson, *The Message* (Colorado Springs: NavPress, 1993).

11 Oswald Chambers, *Daily Thoughts for Disciples* (Nashville: Discovery House, 1994), July 24 entry.

12 Brother Lawrence, *The Practice of the Presence of God* (Springdale, PA: Whitaker House, 1982) p. 21.

13 M. Craig Barnes, *Sacred Thirst* (Grand Rapids: Zondervan, 2001) p. 197.

14 J. B. Phillips, *The New Testament in Modern English* (New York: Macmillan, 1958).

15 John Donne, *Devotions (XVII)* in *John Donne, Selections from Divine Poems, Sermons, Devotions, and Prayers*, edited by John Booty (New York: Paulist Press) p. 271.

16 Amy Carmichael, *Candles in the Dark* (Fort Washington, PA: Christian Literature Crusade) p. 64.

17 George McDonald, *Creation in Christ* (Wheaton, IL: Harold Shaw, 1976) p. 318.

18 Frank Laubach, *Frank, Letters by a Modern Mystic* (Westwood, NJ: Fleming Revell 1937) p. 62.

19 Justin Martyr, *The First Apology*, in *Eerdmans' Book of Christian Classics* (Grand Rapids: Eerdmans Publishing Company, 1985) p. 12.

20 N. T. Wright, *The Lord and His Prayer* (Grand Rapids: Eerdmans Publishing Company, 1996) p. 8.

21 Oswald Chambers, *My Utmost for His Highest* (New York: Dodd, Mead & Company, 1935) p. 291.